ROBERT'S RULES OF REMODELING

A CONSUMER'S GUIDE TO HOME REMODELING
DON'T REMODEL YOUR HOME WITHOUT IT!

ROBERT'S RULES OF REMODELING

A CONSUMER'S GUIDE TO HOME REMODELING
DON'T REMODEL YOUR HOME WITHOUT IT!

ROBERT D. WARREN

Niche Pressworks
Indianapolis

Robert's Rules of Remodeling
ISBN-13: 978-1-946533-29-6

Copyright © 2018 by Robert D. Warren

All rights reserved. No part of this book may be used or reproduced in any manner whatsoever without prior written consent of the author, except as provided by the United States of America copyright law.

Limit of Liability/Disclaimer of Warranty: while the publisher and author have used their best efforts in preparing this book, they make no representations or warranties with respect to the accuracy or completeness of the contents of this book and specifically disclaim any implied warranties of merchantability or fitness for a particular purpose. No warranty may be created or extended by sales representatives or written sales materials. The advice and strategies contained herein may not be suitable for your situation. The publisher or author is not engaged in rendering professional services, and you should consult a professional where appropriate. Neither the publisher nor author shall be liable for any loss of profit or any other commercial damages, including but not limited to special, incidental, consequential, or other damages.

For permission to reprint portions of this content or bulk purchases, contact __Robert@ robertdwarren.com__

Published by Niche Pressworks; http://NichePressworks.com

DEDICATION

To my beautiful and talented wife, Lora, who continues to impart wisdom and discernment. I have learned to take note of what she has to say.

ACKNOWLEDGEMENTS

Thank you to the following who have contributed information and many of the fresh nuggets dispersed throughout this book—Sweet Spots contributors:

Lora Warren

Kim Elrod

Taylor Shutt

Patti Andrews

Meredith Cook

And, to all my current and past clients who have given me the opportunity to serve them throughout the years—thank you!

CONTENTS

Dedication v
Acknowledgements vii
Preface 1
The Curse of Knowledge 5
    Agree on the Terms 5
    Contracts 7
        Lump Sum 7
        Cost Plus 9
    Contractor Profit 10
        Contractor Pricing 10
        Contract Decisions 12
Important Details 15
    Negotiations 15
        Good Sales vs. Bad Sales 15
        Don't be Afraid to Negotiate 16
    Why Is Insurance Important? 17
        General Liability 18
        Workers' Compensation 19
        Proof of Insurance 20
    Warranties 21
        Manufacturer Warranties 21
        Contractor Warranties 22
        Lifetime Warranties 22

The Sales Presentation Process 23
    Finding the Right Contractor 24
        Research 24
        Lead Generation 27
    Phone Interview 28
        Estimates 29
    First Meeting 30
        Promptness 32
    Budget Discussions 33
        Design Deposit 34
    Money Matters 35
    The Contract 37

Kitchens 39
    Assess Your Kitchen Goals 39
    Do Your Homework 40
    Kitchen Layout 40
    Kitchen Style and Cabinet Doors 41
    Cabinet Materials 44
    Cabinet Boxes 45
        Framed Cabinets 45
        European Frameless Cabinets 46
        Drawer Boxes 46
    Finishes 49
    Cabinet Trim 50
    Accessories 52
    Cabinet Hardware 54

- Kitchen Fixtures 55
- Pantry 57
- Outdoor Kitchens 58
- General Project Considerations 58

Bathrooms 61
- Master Bath 62
- Things to Consider in a New Bathroom 63

Cabinet Refacing Explored 71
- About Refacing 71
- Is Refacing Right for You? 72

Countertops 75
- Countertop Options 75

Additions/General Remodeling 79
- Should You Remodel? 79
- Construction Terms 80
- Foundations 81
- Roof Style 83

Lighting and Electrical 87
- Kitchen Lighting 87
- Bathroom Lighting 88
- Family/Living Room Lighting 90
- Bedroom Lighting 90
- Dining Room Lighting 91

Robert's Remedies 93

Thank You 97

Free Consultation 99

About the Author 101
Historic Nuggets from the Past 103
    Old Kitchens 103
    Outdoor "Plumbing" 105
Robert's Rules 107

PREFACE

How many of you have decided on a project for your home only to feel unsure about what to do next? You may have an idea of what you want done or what specific problem needs to be solved, but you're not sure how to go about finding the right person to complete the project for you.

That's one of the reasons I'm writing this book! I want to share my experience in the remodeling business and give you behind-the-scenes information on how to coordinate a successful remodel from start to finish.

The Detail Design philosophy has always been that we do what's best for our clients. While every remodeling project is different, I approach each one with the same goal—to create a space that fits my client's home and makes them happy. That sounds pretty good, right? But, as you may know, remodeling projects can be messy. It's not always easy to translate a plan into action.

That's another one of the reasons I'm writing this book. I get a lot of questions from people about how to make the process go smoothly so I finally decided to put it in writing. I hope to impart some of the things I have learned over the years to help you with your home remodeling project. I want to use my experience to educate you about the remodeling process so that you know what to expect and so that you can make smart decisions.

Basically, this book should help you understand the steps involved in a typical remodeling project. I start by discussing the research and contract phase of a project. While not the most interesting or fun part, it is the most important. It's where you choose who you're going to work with and set down the rules and guidelines for how the project will proceed. That really determines what you're going to get. I then shift to specific types of remodeling projects (like kitchens or bathrooms) and discuss some of the options you'll have.

Throughout the book, I've organized my most essential and useful tips as follows:

- **Robert's Rules** — These are the big ones. The essential nuggets and ideas that you need for a successful project. I set these apart, so you can refer back to them!
- **Robert's Replays** — These are stories from many years in the industry. They describe different types of projects and interactions. These stories are a great way to help explain a point and to make it more memorable. I've changed names and places.
- *The Sweet Spot* — For HGTV and design fans, these spots give insight into popular remodels, trends, and ideas. It's a compilation of "must haves" or "favorites" gathered from decorators and people who are in the process of building a home or doing a large remodel.
- **Lora's Replays** — My wife, Lora. In these spots, she shares her experience and insights.

If you're just at the beginning of the process, the chapters up front provide useful info about what you need to know to get started—picking the right contractor, questions to ask, contracts, etc.

If you've already made the decision to remodel and the actual work is about to start, the later chapters provide details about the specifics of a project—design considerations, finish options, etc.

Let me finish by sharing a story with you. You may have heard it before, but it's useful to remember here.

A lady goes into an auto repair shop to have her car repaired. After checking out the car, the mechanics tell her that she needs a new muffler belt and muffler bearings—neither of which exist! Her lack of knowledge about automobiles makes it possible for them to charge her for something she doesn't need and something they don't need to do. I hope this book helps you better understand the remodeling process, so you know when you're being sold "muffler bearings" and when you're being presented with a legitimate deal.

Now, your first Robert's Replay.

Robert's Replay—Don't Turn Off the Warning Button!

I have a friend who owned a new pickup truck that had the reversing sensors on the bumper. They let you know if you are getting too close to something behind you. The problem with a pickup truck having reverse sensors is that when the tailgate is down it gives you a false alert. So, the car company included a button on the dash that you could push to silence the alarm. This is fine as long as you don't get used to canceling the alarm every time it goes off!

My friend was backing out of a client's driveway one day, and his alarm starting sounding. Of course, he reached over and silenced the alarm because that's what he always did. He then proceeded to back right over their brick mailbox!

Make sure you don't turn off your warning button! If something doesn't seem right, you might do well to go by your gut feelings. This may mean not doing business with someone you're not sure of, or it could be a product selection. Either way, follow your gut instincts.

CHAPTER 1

THE CURSE OF KNOWLEDGE

Have you ever heard of the curse of knowledge? No, it's not a spell somebody casts on you when you're not looking. It's something that's important to understand when you're about to start a project.

You have the curse of knowledge when you know certain things, and you think other people know the same things that you do. To some degree, we all have the curse of knowledge since we bring certain ideas and perspectives to every conversation and interaction. Generally, this is no problem. It makes things interesting!

AGREE ON THE TERMS

But, this curse of knowledge can become a challenge when you're working with someone on a project. Typically, a contractor comes to a project with one understanding of how things progress, and you come to a project with another understanding of how things should progress. You need to recognize these differences and work to define terms and timelines to make sure everyone is talking about the same things—not as easy as it seems.

Agreeing on terms can avoid future problems. Think about this one word—stud. When a carpenter refers to a 2x4 stud (though it's not actually 2" x 4", but 1.5" x 3.5"), it is something made out of wood and used to build things, especially walls. If you refer to a stud when talking to an auto mechanic, they would think of a metal bolt! If you mention a stud to a tailor, they would likely think of something that decorates fabric, while a horse breeder would think of a stallion. One word with many meanings.

I hope I have made my point. When conversing with someone about the specifics of a project, make sure to clarify terms. Because when I say I need to demo your kitchen cabinets, I don't mean demonstrate. I mean demolish!

Basically, every conversation has a lot more going on than you think, and it's important that you and the contractor you're thinking of working with are talking about the same things at the same time! One way to do this is to write things down!

Here are some examples of terms that come up during the initial stages of a project. When you're negotiating details, they're useful to know!

> **Broom clean:** This means the contractor will not be getting out the white glove to make sure he has removed all the dust. If this is a problem with you, then discuss this with the contractor upfront and make sure everyone has the correct expectations.
>
> **We can do that!** If you ask the salesman about a particular item and he says, "We can do that," it doesn't mean he has priced it and put it in the contract! Make sure that if you want something included in the project that you get it written down.

Robert's Replay

I was pricing a kitchen cabinet refacing job when the wife asked if it would be possible to change out a few painted tiles on her white backsplash. I told her it that would be possible and went back to measuring cabinets. I had been working with her husband on the project, and she left after her question.

Nothing more was said about changing those tiles. When we were going over what they wanted done, it wasn't included in the contract. But, while we were there working, she told the guys that I said we would change out the tiles.

I talked with the client about it, and she said she thought I had included it in my price. I went ahead and made the change, but it taught me a valuable lesson.

Make sure all the specifics and details of a project are agreed on by both sides and written down. In this case, I had been talking primarily with the husband, except for the moment his wife came in and asked that question.

I've found that when things don't happen or don't get done, it's usually because they weren't written down! Always get project details in writing. If the contractor promises to do something, it should be in the contract. You want clarity for everyone.

Robert's Rule #1

If it's not in writing, it is not clear. Make sure the contract contains everything you discussed. Review the contract before signing. If it's unclear about anything, then have it revised so it covers what you want done, and, only then, should you sign it.

CONTRACTS

Contracts and an agreed upon payment structure are another area where the curse of knowledge needs to be avoided. Contractors typically use two types of contracts—lump sum and cost plus. Let's look at them in greater detail

Lump Sum

First, let's cover my preferred contract method—lump sum payment agreements. These are, by far, the most common contracts used by contractors. Essentially, the contractor prices a job based upon a project's scope as well as the specific materials or material allowances needed. Everything is included in a single lump sum amount.

This type of contract puts the risk on the contractor—which is what you want! If the contractor estimates it will take 100 hours to complete a job and it actually takes 110 hours, then they bear the extra cost and not you. As always, it is essential to remember that if there is a change to a project's scope or material selections, then be sure to get an updated agreement that details the changes and the new project pricing.

If you have a lump sum contract, make sure all details are included in the scope of work. This includes making sure you have a very detailed list of the items needed to complete the project as well as pretty accurate dollar amounts for each of these items. You may even choose to go into greater detail by including specific model numbers for certain items.

Let's think about a typical bathroom remodel. For this project, your item list would need to include: tiles, a sink, a vanity, shower valve and trim, countertops, light fixtures, and a toilet. You can structure the contract by having a general allowance number for everything, a specific list of items with model numbers and amounts, or a combination of the two. Whatever option you choose, make sure the information is detailed and included in the contract.

Robert's Rule #2

Never use the contractors' financing without first checking on financing from your own bank. Or, pay cash. A twelve-month same as cash deal could cost the contractor hundreds of dollars, and he will charge that into the job and have you think he is doing you a favor.

Cost Plus

I generally avoid cost-plus contracts, but they can be useful when you want a lot of control over a contractor's work and/or you want project flexibility. With this type of contract, you tell the contractor what needs to be done (and maybe outline a plan).

You cover the project's actual expenses (including all materials and labor) plus other costs required to complete the project. The plus part is typically a fixed fee agreed upon with the contractor that covers the contractor's overhead and profit. In a cost-plus contract, you are the project manager, so you track purchases and project management. This can be a benefit or a drawback.

A disadvantage of the cost-plus contract is that the final cost is uncertain. Some think you're even giving the contractor an incentive to have cost overruns because the higher the project costs, the more the contractor makes.

I prefer lump sum contracts. In my experience, cost-plus contracts can be bad for homeowners because they don't give contractors any incentive to control costs. They can be bad for contractors because if they don't monitor their costs carefully, they could lose their profit margin. I see it as a risky deal for both sides.

Robert's Rule #3

Think long and hard before agreeing to a cost-plus contract. This payment structure can give the contractor an incentive to spend more, because with every dollar he spends he gets his percentage. In contrast, a fixed amount contract gives the contractor an incentive not to overspend.

CONTRACTOR PROFIT

Don't get nervous when I mention contractor profit, as I do in the contracts section. It's an important piece of the remodeling puzzle. Successful contractors are able to work with you to find a price that you're happy with and a price that makes them a profit. It's good business for everyone to find a balance between cost and value. Let me give you a behind-the-scenes perspective on pricing and profit from a contractor's perspective.

The important thing is that the contractor needs to make a profit, so they can stay in business. This ensures that they're around to take care of any warranty issues, and any future projects you may need. Some people may think that contractors are making a killing on every job. The truth is, many contractors do not make a great deal of profit on projects. This can happen because they don't know how to estimate accurately or simply because they love their building work and don't love the work of running a business. In either case, it can be easy to lose money as a contractor.

While it's not your job to ensure that contractors stay in business, it is a good idea to understand the costs of a professional contracting business. These include worker's compensation, insurance, office management, and materials. The prices charged need to cover these costs, so contractors rely on markups and margins when setting prices.

Contractor Pricing

A markup is how much more than the purchase price a contractor charges for an item. For instance, if a sink costs them $20, they might charge a homeowner $40. This additional cost helps pay for insurance, labor, and maybe even office management. The markup helps them meet their margin, or profit. They need to make a certain amount on each project to make staying in business worthwhile and profitable.

A contractor won't give you an itemized breakdown that includes overhead and profit. That's behind-the-scenes business. But, rest assured, there is something that keeps contractors from charging too much—competition!

That's right! As consumers, we have the right to do business with anyone. If a contractor charges too much without giving the right services and the right value, customers will stop using them. If one contractor provides better service or quality at a better rate, then you will certainly choose that person. Competitors will need to figure out how to match that quality and price.

Keep in mind that there are many types of contractors to choose from, ranging from repair service companies that charge by the hour to specialized kitchen and bath contractors. The contractor you hire depends on the type of work you want done and your budget.

If you want to hire a professional contractor who is insured and properly licensed, you will have to pay a professional price. Other companies (some call them "Chuck and A Truck" operations) typically cut costs by cutting corners. They may not have insurance or a contractor's license, and good luck tracking them down if something goes wrong.

There are three ways to lower the price of a job.

1. Scope of work (one bathroom or two)
2. Selection of material (tile floor or laminate floor)
3. Homeowner involvement (you might feel comfortable doing the painting to save some money)

Each of these can lower the price of a project. Otherwise, if the contractor has priced everything correctly and hasn't missed anything, he won't have much wiggle room on price.

Finally, consider who you're hiring for your job. There are many types of contractors with different specialties. It's important to choose the right person for the job.

- Handyman and repair service companies usually charge by the hour and do small jobs. These contractors tend to have the highest markups because they have the highest overhead, and many times are providing emergency repairs.

- Specialty contractors (window and siding replacement, roofing contractors, and gutter companies) have a high markup because they spend a high percentage of their income on advertising. You will hear these types of commercials on the radio and get tired of them.
- Kitchen/bath contractors and closet companies have a lower markup because they don't advertise as much and have lower overhead costs.
- Larger remodelers who do whole house remodels and larger additions tend to have the lowest overhead as a percentage. They typically have superintendents and mostly hire subcontractors to complete the work.

Robert's Rule #4

Never make a decision to use a contractor based on money. Much of the time, you will be wrong. Money is the worst indicator of honesty, integrity, quality of work, a successful project, etc.

Contract Decisions

When starting your remodeling process and looking at contracts, think about the things I've discussed in this chapter.

- Discuss and agree on specifics.
- Write it down.
- Decide on contract structure.
- Consider contractor cost to value.

If you keep these things in mind, you'll find a balance between cost and value. Now, let's look at how to get the most out of your contract.

Robert's Replay

One client was a retired professor. She called and set up an appointment for me to come out and discuss a new kitchen. I designed the kitchen based on her input and budget. We had several options she wanted me to price up as well. She had her friend at each meeting when we discussed the pricing. As we discussed the options, she decided she couldn't afford some of them, so we didn't include those in the contract.

Dealing with Clients with Memory Loss

We have had several projects where clients' memory problems have made communicating difficult.

After a few weeks, we were installing the kitchen and she told my installers that she was supposed to get the options we discussed. I had to talk with her about this, and she finally understood, but it was obvious she didn't remember. I had to refer her back to the contract and reminded her that her friend was present when we decided not to do the options. Upon completion of the project, my installers told me there were several times she would ask something and later ask the same thing over.

If you have a spouse, parent, or relative that is starting to show signs of memory loss, make sure your contractor is aware of it. If we know about it, we can take safeguards to make sure we don't end up in a misunderstanding. Try to make sure they don't make an agreement with a contractor without your input. Also, if there are other selections to be made, it is a good idea to accompany them and write down their choices.

CHAPTER 2
IMPORTANT DETAILS

NEGOTIATIONS

I was riding in the car with my wife one day listening to the radio. They were about to go to a commercial break and before they did they said, "When we get back, we will tell you the seven most powerful words in the English language!" This piqued my interest. Before the commercial was over, I said to my wife, "They're going to say: Is that the best you can do?" She didn't think that was right, but when the radio host came back on that is exactly what they said.

This got me thinking more about negotiating. Why do we negotiate? What skills are needed to be a good negotiator? Why wouldn't we negotiate? I feel like it comes back to feeling like we are "being sold." Nobody likes to feel like they have been taken advantage of.

Good Sales vs. Bad Sales

Yet many times when we deal with a salesperson that's what we feel like. I think it's because we often enter a negotiation without as much information or expertise as the person doing the selling. You know how you want your completed remodel to look, but you may not know the code requirements or specific materials to get you to that end result. You may feel a little out of your element when discussing these very specific details. Add in a pushy salesperson, and you may start to feel frustrated.

A good salesperson should have the heart of a teacher and be able to listen more than they talk. You should feel that your ideas are being heard so that they can figure out what the problem truly is and come up with the best solution for you.

I took a sales training program and this story stuck with me:

A salesperson is selling packaging for meat markets. He comes in and asks the meat market manager if he would consider using their company for their packaging needs.

The manager asked him if they put coupons on the packaging. The salesperson answered, "Oh yes!" He then proceeded to spend 10 minutes telling him about all the different kinds of coupons they could put on his packaging.

As soon as he stopped talking, the meat market manager said, "Oh, that's too bad. I don't like coupons on my packaging."

That salesperson should have spent more time listening to find out the manager's true needs.

Robert's Rule #5

Before signing the deal, ask a contractor the seven most powerful words in the English language—"Is that the best you can do?"

Don't be Afraid to Negotiate

Negotiating is not something Americans do very often. Many times, we prefer to know the price of an item or service and just pay that set fee. No haggling; no playing games. But, in many other cultures, if you don't negotiate, they will feel slighted. In some cultures, negotiation happens until a project is completed, even though you have a signed contract for the agreed upon amount. While I'm not advocating for that, I do think negotiating is important.

In the US, negotiations are done at the start of a project. After the contract is signed, you can't then ask for a better deal. Negotiating also shouldn't be about trying to get something for nothing. It's really just a way to get a fair price.

There have been times I haven't asked for lower prices and thought later that maybe I should have. There have also been times when I asked for a discount (even in a department store), and the clerk gave me a percentage off. Asking for a discounted price does not mean you are taking advantage of the salesperson or the company. You are just working to get the best deal. Be reasonable.

Robert's Replay

I have a friend who frequents garage sales—where everything is negotiable! She once found something she was really interested in, and the seller said, "Please don't ask me to lower the price because that's as low as I can go." Our friend responded, "I won't. I know this is very reasonable."

You want to be that person who knows the value of something and who knows when to stop negotiating.

Robert's Rule #6

Negotiate, but be reasonable. Be Nice.

WHY IS INSURANCE IMPORTANT?

You found your contractor, agreed upon terms, negotiated price and project details, so now you can get started, right? No! Don't forget an extremely important part of any remodeling project—insurance. It doesn't sound very interesting or fun, but it protects both you and your contractor.

Insurance basically protects you by limiting your risk. Think of it this way, you have auto insurance to cover you in the event of an accident. It limits your financial exposure to just your deductible and policy limits. For instance, if you have an accident and create $100,000 in damages, you don't pay $100,000. You only pay your deductible amount (usually $500 to $2,500) and the insurance company pays up to your policy limit. Of course, this is better than writing a check for $100,000.

Every professional contractor should have two types of insurance coverage—General Liability and Workers' Compensation. Because having this type of insurance coverage is expensive and a big benefit for homeowners, contractors with proper insurance tend to charge higher prices than your local "Chuck and A Truck" companies.

Let me help you understand why these two types of insurance are important by explaining how each type of insurance coverage benefits both you and your contractor.

General Liability

What would you do if the contractor accidentally burned your house down while working on it? What would happen if the contractor accidentally flooded the house? If there is a terrible accident during your project, a general liability policy covers it. I'm not an insurance expert, but I think you get the idea. This type of insurance covers you for most liabilities or accidents. If your contractor has it, then you essentially have it too!

What could happen if you don't use a contractor with this type of insurance? Let's say you hire "Chuck and A Truck" to clean your gutters. You notice his aluminum ladder looks like it was run over because one side is crushed!

He leans the ladder against the house, extends it 25 feet, and climbs up to clean the gutters. As he leans further over, the ladder foot breaks, and the ladder starts falling. The contractor falls off the ladder and lands head first on your driveway. The paramedics arrive and take him away.

You think everything is over. But, before you know it, a lawyer has contacted you about a lawsuit against you for a few million dollars because of this accident.

Here is where it can get ugly. Most people do not have a homeowner's policy over one million dollars. If this guy wins in court, your homeowner's policy will only cover up to the limit. Anything above that (maybe millions!) will come from your assets and future income. All because you wanted to save a few dollars and not use a licensed and insured contractor.

Use wisdom. Peace of mind is worth paying for!

Robert's Rule #7

Talk with your insurance agent before embarking on a new remodeling project. They will make sure you are properly covered.

Workers' Compensation

This insurance is designed to cover a worker who gets injured on the job. Let's say you hire "Chuck and A Truck" again. This time, he accidentally cuts himself very badly, and you have to take him to the hospital. This could easily be a $300,000 injury claim.

If your contractor carries workers' compensation insurance (like he is supposed to) then this type of accident will be covered. If Chuck doesn't have this insurance, then it will probably go to your homeowner's insurance which may exclude workers' compensation claims. If this is the case, you will have the privilege of experiencing our justice system while defending yourself against this claim.

Again, peace of mind is worth paying for!

Proof of Insurance

Now that you realize the importance of insurance, you realize the stakes are high. Always ask to have your contractor's insurance company send you a copy of their workers' compensation and general liability certificates—directly from the agent to your house. Never rely on a photocopy of an insurance certificate. It is too easy to counterfeit!

Robert's Rule #8

Always have your contractor send a copy of insurance coverage directly from the insurance agent. DO NOT accept a photocopy!

Robert's Replay

Many years ago, I hired a roofing subcontractor for some of our roofing jobs. He brought me his certificate of insurance for my records, but, after a few weeks, we found out he had taken an expired certificate and altered it. We were writing checks out to the name on the certificate, and he was cashing them, but he wasn't legitimately insured, putting both my clients and my company at risk.

That is when I learned you never take a photocopy of a certificate. You always have it sent directly to you from their insurance company. You should also get the insurance certificate at least one day before starting your project. It won't go into effect until the next day after it is issued by the insurance company.

Robert's Rule #9

Never start a project on the same day the insurance certificate is issued. The certificate will have the issue date, but it won't go into effect until the next day.

WARRANTIES

Since we're covering important project details, we need to discuss warranties.

Manufacturer Warranties

Manufacturer warranties tend to last one year for most products, but you have to read the fine print to be sure! A good warranty is backed by the strength of the company selling it and the strength of the company making it. Companies that have good-quality products typically stand behind a product if you have problems.

But, before committing to a big purchase, take some time to look at product reviews. These can be a great way to see what other people say about a product you are considering and help you decide if the product is a good fit for your needs. Reviews can also be a good indicator of product quality and/or how the company handles returns.

Asbestos and Lead Paint

Houses built before 1978 have a greater possibility of containing asbestos. Paint, flooring, siding, insulation, and shingles are just some of the items that have been made with asbestos. Asbestos is a very toxic material when it becomes airborne and is then inhaled.

Also, when houses were painted with lead paint, a child could chew on the wood, ingest the chemicals, and be harmed. If you have a house built before the 1980s, you might want to take extra precaution and have it checked for asbestos and/or lead-based paint.

Robert's Rule #10

There is no such thing as a lifetime warranty. (Well, almost never.) If you don't believe me, just read the fine print. Most cabinet lifetime warranties are for seven to ten years.

Ask yourself—if you were selling a product, under what circumstances would you be willing to offer a lifetime warranty? It may only be a sales gimmick.

Contractor Warranties

Contractor warranties also vary, but a one-year warranty is pretty standard in the industry. The state of Georgia requires contractors to give at least one year of warranty coverage. In this situation, the manufacturer's warranties cover the product, and the contractor's warranty covers the installation. Your contract usually will spell out specific warranty terms.

Take note: if you purchase an item for the contractor to install, and it then goes bad under warranty, you will have to pay the contractor to remove the defective part and install the new part. If you have the contractor provide the product, they will be responsible if it needs replacement.

On any big-ticket items, you should keep the purchase receipt and the warranty information with your important papers. That way, if something comes up later, you can find it. These items tend to have longer warranties even if they are limited.

Lifetime Warranties

There aren't many true lifetime warranties out there. Craftsman tools used to have a true lifetime warranty so that if one of their tools broke they would replace it for free. Usually, a lifetime warranty claim is so limited it turns out to be more of a marketing scheme, so beware when you see it. We have a competitor to the Detail Cabinet Refacing division of our company who advertises a lifetime warranty. But, we have been called out to repair some of their projects that were poorly installed and built when they would not repair them for the client. So much for a lifetime warranty.

CHAPTER 3

THE SALES PRESENTATION PROCESS

Let's talk about that word—sales—or salesperson. Many people conjure up an image of a shady, used car salesman with suspenders and a cigar, pushing you into something you don't want or need. Unfortunately, that still happens. What should you look for in a contractor to keep this from happening to you? Let's look at the overall process to see.

You wake up one Saturday morning and tell your spouse, "Let's remodel the kitchen today!" No, that probably never happens. Our clients typically spend 1.5 to 2 years thinking about and planning their project before actually starting it. That's a long time.

Here's what I suggest. Before you start any remodeling project, do two things—educate yourself about the process and, take your time! By reading this book, you're already on your way to understanding how the process will work. Now, you need to focus on taking your time to find the right contractor.

Don't make impulsive decisions when it comes to home remodeling projects. Finding the right contractor is more than finding someone who can do the work. It's about finding someone you can work with who understands the remodeling project you want done. Let's look at the steps that will get you to that person.

FINDING THE RIGHT CONTRACTOR

You have been planning your project or putting up with the pain of an ugly kitchen for several years, and you've finally decided it is time to start moving forward with the process. This is where you start becoming aware of contractors.

You might start looking online, reading reviews, and/or asking friends for recommendations as you try to come up with some companies that you can talk to. All these are good places to start, but my first recommendation is to do your homework before you start calling contractors. Check them out online (that means looking at their website and review sites). Look at pictures of other projects they have worked on and see what others are saying about them.

Things to Watch Out For

Some contractors try to sell homeowners something they don't need. Using a dazzling performance, they try to convince someone that they need a product that may be overrated and/or overpriced. Remember—if someone is flattering you, they may not have your best interest in mind.

Another tactic to watch out for is a steep discount for signing today. Be careful in this situation because they may be trying to close the deal without giving you time to think about it. A small discount if you sign today is not unusual—especially if the contractor is trying to fill a hole in his schedule—but a big discount for signing quickly should set off alarms!

What you are looking for is a feel for their company philosophy. Are they focused on taking care of their clients or are they focused on taking care of themselves? This will show up in the reviews and possibly in other statements (or lack thereof) about their company—rude salespeople, poor service, little or no warranty response.

Anyone can have a bad day, but it's how they recover and treat their clients in tough situations that counts.

Research

When I was a kid, the technology we use today was only in the movies. Remember the television show *Get Smart?* The secret agent had a phone in his shoe! Or what about *Mission Impossible?* They always had cool gadgets. Just as technology has changed so has the way we find contractors.

But, even with all of this technology, you're still looking for many of the same qualities in a contractor. Now, it's just easier to research and get information about a potential contractor.

Robert's Rule #11

Don't use a contractor who doesn't have a good website. It should be more than just a basic website. It should be up to date, mobile optimized, and have enough information about the business to get a feeling about whether you would want to use them. A good website with these items costs money to be maintained and shows commitment to their business.

There are quite a few online sources where you can find service providers and read reviews about them. I recommend that you use sites that have been around for a while with proven track records. In several states, Kudzu.com is a great resource, and everyone has access to Houzz.com. These types of resources give you access to contractors in your region as well as brief reviews of their work.

Once you've found a few sites, you can start looking for someone that does what you are looking for. Start a list of contractors in your area who seem like good possibilities for your particular project (maybe they specialize in kitchen remodels or half-bath renovations). Read about each of them, look at their pictures, look at their website, and get a feel for both the contractor and their philosophy. It should all be there. You just have to look for it.

Read their reviews—the good and the bad. You will see how the company responds to a client, which tells you a lot about them. You will also see, based on some of the reviews, that there are some crazy people out there.

I try to avoid sites that do not allow service providers to respond or comment on reviews. If someone has had a bad experience, it's best to let both sides present their perspective. Oftentimes, when people are upset about something and vent their emotions via a bad review, the contractor and client just need to communicate. Usually, a good contractor contacts them about the matter and works to resolve it. In those situations, a bad review can become a good review, and you have good information about how they handle disagreements.

Robert's Rule #12

It's not how you mess up, but how you recover that counts! Everyone makes mistakes. That's a fact.

When you are doing a multi-faceted project, there is always room for something not to go as planned. A person's character is observed by how they deal with that situation. Don't judge a contractor by a problem that may come up, but by how it gets taken care of. There are many variables, and it may not have been something he did.

Remember, you are looking for someone you want to do business with for possibly the next two to five months, depending on the size of the job. Make sure you like them. I have talked with people who did business with contractors just because they were the lowest bidder, even though they disliked them from the beginning! Needless to say, by the end of the project they would have paid the higher price not to have to go through what they did. You will find that if you do your homework and select a good contractor (who is a good fit for both you and your project), the end result will be much better.

Robert's Replay

One potential client called me to look at an addition she wanted to build across the back of her house. When I got there, we walked into the den, and you could see out the back windows that someone had already started building something.

She said, "I guess you can see my problem!" I said, "Not really, what is it?" She proceeded to tell me that she had hired a contractor to do an addition, and he had made a mess of it. She said he came highly recommended by a neighbor. I asked who the contractor was, and she said it was So-and-So Painting and Remodeling.

The problem was that he was a painter who did some light remodeling. Additions were probably out of his league. I have sewn buttons on my shirt, and I'm certain I could sew a button on your shirt that would stay on. But, do not ask me to *make you the shirt*—I would make a mess of it, but the buttons would be on tight! It's important to choose a contractor who has completed projects of similar size and scope to yours. It's much more expensive and tiresome when you need to change contractors during a project.

Robert's Rule #13

Choose a contractor with experience in the specific type of project that you have. For example, don't choose John's Painting for a kitchen remodel or Joe's Plumbing to complete bathroom renovation. You want every detail done well.

Lead Generation

Things have really changed in the last 15 to 20 years. There was a time when contractors would pay big dollars to be listed in the yellow pages. That was where many people first went to find a contractor. I would venture to say that some people reading this have never used the yellow pages or maybe never even seen a pay phone!

As you begin your search for a contractor, you will inevitably go online. A word of caution—beware of service provider websites that are vague about the services offered, but still request your personal information. Many contractors get new business by using lead generation companies. These are directories and media sites (Angie's List, HomeAdvisor, Yellow Pages) where a contractor pays to list their information. It's a form of marketing that our company doesn't use.

Once a lead generation company gets your information, you are likely to be bombarded with emails or calls from companies you've never heard of trying to set up an appointment to meet with you.

At Detail Design and Remodeling, we choose to market our services ourselves. If you see one of our ads and click on it, it takes you straight to our website where you can learn more about us. If you call the number listed, it will go straight to our office. We prefer this direct interaction with our clients, and most of our clients prefer it too.

However, don't be alarmed if you see one phone number in a company's ad, and another phone number listed on their website. Many companies (including us) use tracking phone numbers with their advertisements. These phone numbers are used in specific advertisements and let us know where people have heard about us and which of our ads led you to us.

PHONE INTERVIEW

After you create a list of companies you are interested in, your next step is to narrow the list by calling and talking to five or so possibilities. Too many people overlook the phone interview and have companies come out to look at their project before they know whether or not it's even a good fit.

Save yourself (and the contractors) some time by talking to them for 15–20 minutes to see what their strengths are and the type of projects they like to do. You may find out that some don't like to do the type of project you want to do, some won't call you back, and some will be too busy to meet with you right now. If a contractor seems uninterested, don't waste their time or yours. Find someone who is interested in you.

During the phone interview, you should also think about how they interact with you. How did they answer the phone and respond to your questions? If they are rude and short on the phone, it probably won't get any better later. A good remodeler will already have a process in place to take you through some questions about your project to see if you are a good fit for each other.

Robert's Rule #14

Never do business with someone you don't like. Even if they have the lowest price—you may end up regretting it!

Note: Don't ask for references during this initial phone call! Contractors prefer to provide references later in the process after they have met with you, and you've both determined whether the project is a good fit.

After talking with contractors on your list, narrow your choices down to one or two. After they give you a price for the scope of work and right before you sign a contract with them, ask for a few references. This should confirm that you are right to hire them.

Estimates

Regardless of what you have heard, **DO NOT GET TOO MANY ESTIMATES!** It leads to confusion and, in the long run, doesn't help. Don't overwhelm yourself.

How many estimates should you get? Ideally, you should not get more than two (three at the most) estimates for a project. Any more than that and it gets confusing.

Robert's Rule #15

Do not get too many estimates! It will lead to paralysis of analysis! The estimates are unlikely to include the exact same products or solutions, and too many can get overwhelming.

Robert's Replay

I had a kitchen client one time ask me why he shouldn't be getting a lot more estimates. His reasoning was that having a lot of other prices would help him make sure my price was in line. The problem with that logic is that each contractor approaches a project differently. Three estimates from three different contractors only gives you the cost of three different projects because it is almost impossible to get all three on the same page!

I had been working with this client about three weeks, and we had discussed it in great detail. I felt I had captured what he wanted perfectly. So, I asked him before he saw my final price what he thought it was going to be. He did, and he was within $300 on a $40,000 kitchen job. The point being, he already had a good idea what it was worth and was comfortable with me and my company.

FIRST MEETING

Now that you have found companies you feel comfortable with, it's time for face-to-face meetings. This needs to be at your house, so they can see your project in person. When you set up this appointment, find out what the contractor or sales consultant wants to accomplish during this visit so you can be prepared.

That might mean having a written wish list for the project or specifics about problems you currently have with your space. You should also prepare questions for the contractor to get an idea of how they approach projects. It's also a great time to get design or layout suggestions from the contractor.

When the company representative arrives, remember you are interviewing each other. You are looking for clues that might lead to a great relationship or a bad one. At this point, let the contractor lead the meeting. If they have the heart of a true professional, they will want you to do most of the talking (70% you and 30% them) to find out your needs and desires. If you encounter just an average contractor, they will do all the talking and try to sell you what they are selling.

Robert's Rule #16

A true professional will spend time listening to what you have to say.

Think about a visit with your doctor. Most physicians will ask you questions about your health or your pain and have you do most of the talking. They will spend little time talking about themselves.

To help figure out your needs, the doctor needs to listen to you in order to get enough information to do that. Likewise, a contractor needs to listen to you talk about the project to get enough information to make a plan that suits you.

If a contractor does all the talking during your first meeting, they may not be the best fit. It tells you they are more interested in selling you what they have than finding out what you need.

I would also be wary of a contractor who demands every meeting be at their office. Usually, they will have the first meeting at your home to get pictures and measurements and then may want you to come to their office. That's fine if you are okay with it, but usually they do this to control the process and have the home-team advantage.

Robert's Rule #17

When setting up the first meeting for a sales consultation, note how this initial part of the process goes. First impressions can be very telling. It might help you decide whether or not to use them later on.

Promptness

During a project, I encourage both parties to be mindful and courteous about meeting times. Everyone is busy so it's important to arrive on time (if not a little early) and to phone if a delay is expected (due to traffic or an earlier appointment running late). I make a point of having my office confirm appointments one day before, and I call ahead of the scheduled time to let clients know I'm on the way.

Robert's Replay

One time, a gentleman referred by another client called saying he needed to meet very quickly, like that same day. Our scheduler worked to fit it in at a time that suited him. I arrived on time, and he wasn't there. His wife called to let him know I was there, and he said he was on his way.

We expected him soon, since he worked only five minutes away. I measured and did everything I could do ahead of our meeting. Out of respect for my previous client who had referred him, I waited. His wife called him two more times over the course of an hour and a half—she was so embarrassed!

He finally showed up, and I completed the sales consultation and left. But, I lost time I could have spent helping other clients and left thinking that we may not be a good fit. Not my favorite conclusion, but something to consider during the early stages of a project.

Robert's Rule #18

Be courteous! If you need to reschedule an appointment, call the salesperson. If you cannot reach them, call the company directly. Do for them what you would want them to do for you!

BUDGET DISCUSSIONS

Don't be afraid to talk about your budget! Let me say that again in a different way—know your budget and let your contractor know it too! It can be tough to talk about money, but it's the only way a contractor can create a plan that meets your needs.

A good contractor will want to hear your thoughts about what you want—the scope of the project, different types of materials, timelines, etc.—and how much you want to spend. What you want may give them a general budget range for your project. Or, it may mean they need to talk to you about what your budget can do.

While some people are afraid to give their target budget, they need to remember that this is an essential piece of the planning discussion, and it ensures that the contractor and you are in the same universe.

For example, take a new car buying experience. You walk into a dealership that sells Mercedes, VWs, and Hondas. If you tell the salesperson you don't know what your budget is, he might show you a $100,000 Mercedes! If you're really thinking around $20,000, you need to let the salesperson know so they can show you something in your range. The same thing is true for contractors!

Robert's Replay

Let me describe a typical budget conversation during the initial phase of a project. I was starting a new kitchen project and asked the couple about their budget.

They replied, "We don't know." So, I asked, "Are you okay spending $80,000 on this?" Their surprised response was, "Oh no, not that much!" I then asked, "How about $50,000?" They responded, "No. We were thinking about $20,000 or so." So, I said, "$20,000 to $25,000 is a safe range?" They agreed, "Yes, but certainly not $30,000."

I drew up the plan we discussed and priced it. It was a little more than they wanted to spend. As a result of our budget discussion, I was able to come up with a few options to save them some money. We eliminated some lighting and got the price down to about $23,000.

Another purpose of the budget discussion is to keep everyone from wasting time on a $50,000 kitchen plan when the budget is really $10,000! If you feel comfortable with the contractor and the company, you should feel comfortable sharing a budget range.

Design Deposit

Some kitchen and bath contractors require a design deposit (or feasibility study) before going beyond the discussion phase. This isn't unusual, but make sure you know exactly what you are getting for that money. And, ask if this fee will be applied to the job if you decide to move forward with them (usually it is!).

Robert's Rule #19

If you are creatively challenged, then make sure you hire the services of someone who can help you with ideas and viable options. Someone who can help you with aesthetic and color options. I have worked with many decorators and designers who turn out great work and are usually reasonably priced.

Some contractors call the design deposit a trial close. Their reasoning is that if the client is willing to put down about $1,500 for a design, then they are probably willing to move forward with a $50,000 remodel.

My philosophy on this depends on the project. If I can draw and price a project up in three to four hours, I usually don't require a deposit upfront. If a client wants a more complicated design that will take me several days to design, then I usually require a deposit. You have to recognize the value a professional brings to a project and how beneficial it is for you to have them involved in the early design stages.

After the first meeting, the contractor will spend a week or so drawing and pricing up your project based on your input at the first meeting and your budget. I usually do several design ideas to show my clients, but I only price up the one I like the best. This gives us a good starting point, and we can tweak it from there.

At this point, the contractor sets up a second meeting to review ideas and go over the pricing. You will likely discuss material selections and allowances. Sometimes it takes two or three meetings to get all the details worked out just right.

> ### Robert's Rule #20
>
> At the end of each visit, always set up the next appointment day and time and agree about the purpose of the next meeting and its anticipated outcome.

MONEY MATTERS

Once you've decided to move forward with a contractor, most, if not all, will require an initial deposit (separate from the design deposit) and then additional payments that are scheduled at specific points during the project. This allows the contractor to complete your project without becoming your banker.

Usually when someone says you don't have to pay until the work is done, they do small jobs or use finance companies. The finance companies typically pay the contractor upfront, though you may think they are not getting paid until they are finished.

> **Robert's Rule #21**
>
> Caution: Don't give a subcontractor money upfront. Only pay in full when a project is completed.
>
> A general contractor is licensed and insured and is usually well established. For general contractors, it is standard to get an upfront deposit and additional payments throughout the project.

I recommend scheduling follow-up payments at the start of a new project phase, not the end. It can be difficult to determine if something is finished, but it's very easy to see if something is starting.

After signing the contract and writing a deposit check, the company should follow up with you about the schedule and any selections that still need to be made. It is in your best interest to make all your selections as soon as possible so as to not slow down progress.

Here are some essential terms to know when setting up the payment portion of an agreement.

Allowance: In the contract, the contractor sets aside a certain amount of money (the allowance) for materials needed during the project. They will either stay within a certain price range for an item or have a specific price for a specific item, like a Kohler Cimarron toilet. If you vary from this allowance, you may owe additional money or, if you choose something that costs less, you may have a credit coming.

Owner participation: This is one of three ways to lower the price of a remodeling job. Exact details about owner participation should be written into the contract. For instance, it could say that the owner will remove and dispose of the countertops. The other two ways to lower the price of a remodel would be to select less expensive materials or to change the scope of the project.

Final Payment: This is the point where you go over the job with the contractor and create a final list of things for them to correct (we call this the punch list). The contract should be structured to have this final payment due at completion. On a larger job, I usually request $1,500. On a smaller job, it might be the second half of the total.

After you and the contractor agree that the project has been completed and any final repairs have been made, you should go ahead and make the final payment. Anything that comes up after this would be part of the contractor's warranty. All good contractors are going to take care of your warranty needs because they know that if you are happy, you are going to refer them to others.

THE CONTRACT

By this time, you have done your homework, agreed on terms, and you feel comfortable with the contractor, their company, and their ideas. Now, it is time to enter into a contract with them to produce the project you have been planning and anticipating for a while.

Every contract has legalese language in it. Make sure the contract meets the needs of both sides and is not heavily weighted in favor of the contractor. Beware if you read it and notice that it only talks about what happens if you don't do something and says nothing about what happens if the contractor doesn't do something. Don't be afraid to make changes to the contract. As Zig Ziglar used to say, "You can't make a good deal with a bad guy!"

Robert's Rule #22

Zig Ziglar used to say, "You can't make a good deal with a bad guy." Character matters!

Make sure everything you discuss is in writing. This benefits both you and your contractor. If it's not in writing, it won't happen! Take particular care when reviewing both the contract and any drawings. Be sure to have the contractor explain things in detail so you have another chance to be sure you're talking about the same thing. You don't want the curse of knowledge to strike! If something is missing or unclear, talk about it and resolve it now. Make sure all the changes are made before signing the contract.

Now, you're ready for the fun part of the project. Thinking about all the possibilities for your space.

Reality TV Fans—Beware!

Reality television is entertainment! It's fun to watch and get design ideas from these shows, but keep the following in mind while watching.

Time frame: Most of these projects are filmed over several weeks and edited to look as if completed in a shorter timeframe. The ones that are actually completed in the timeframe indicated are using an unrealistic number of workers to complete the project in a very short timeframe. This keeps it entertaining and workable for TV, but, in the real world, this would make your project so expensive you wouldn't want to do it!

Budget: Many of the budget numbers on these shows are not very realistic either. Keep in mind that the show is looking for people who will donate their time or material to be on TV.

Pictures: You have to be careful about relying on things you see in pictures or on a TV show. They tend to look better on TV than in person. The colors are hard to get exact as well. Just keep in mind these shows have great editing abilities.

Preparation: These shows can spend months preparing for the project seen on TV that is being completed in a week!

Use these shows for ideas and, of course, for great entertainment! Beyond that, they are a Not-Quite-Reality TV.

CHAPTER 4

KITCHENS

The kitchen is the cornerstone of the house. It's usually the gathering room. People often make major decisions in the kitchen. Plans are made, and bonding takes place. This is the place where your day starts!

Because of the importance of this space, we can't overemphasize the value of careful planning when considering a kitchen remodel. A kitchen can either help or hurt the sale of a house. It can either increase or decrease a home's value. Therefore, you have to really make sure that your plan is going to help and not hurt the value of the home.

ASSESS YOUR KITCHEN GOALS

When I'm approached about a possible kitchen remodel, I always ask people about their overall goals for a new kitchen. How long are they planning to stay in the house? Are they just trying to get the house ready to sell in the near future? Or, do they want to upgrade for their own enjoyment?

If you're thinking you are going to stay in the house long-term, you have more options because you don't have to be concerned with how your design choices will affect whether or not the house sells.

You may have always wanted to do a rustic kitchen, but your house is very traditional. Maybe you think a dishwasher is not needed, or you don't like using a microwave, so you don't include those in the kitchen plan. Normally, this would be a mistake. But, if you are going to stay in the house forever, it won't matter until your heirs inherit the house and either have to pay to remodel the kitchen before selling or take a lesser price so the new buyer can make the upgrades.

Are you planning to sell soon? If so, the kitchen design plan requires more thought. You'll want to focus on what the buyers might want and keep things more neutral. Make sure the kitchen matches the style of the house. If you have a traditional style home, buyers are likely to expect a traditional (not contemporary) style kitchen.

If you are going to sell in the next five years you have a little more flexibility, but you still need to consider what a buyer might want and not go too wild.

DO YOUR HOMEWORK

Doing a full kitchen remodel is a big commitment, both in time and money, so you want to make sure you're prepared. There are lots of decisions that have to be made—many before the demolition of the existing kitchen even begins.

Below, we'll give you an overview of the things you need to think about, and a description of some of the options you have in space design/layout, cabinet wood, style, trims, finishes, and amenities.

KITCHEN LAYOUT

The thing most people think about with a kitchen remodel is that when finished, everything will be shiny and new. But, if you are going to live through the construction, you should also consider whether improvements can be made in the organization of the kitchen to increase efficiency. This is an opportunity to maybe change the location of the sink, ovens, or even refrigerator.

The National Kitchen and Bath Association (NKBA) has guidelines for optimizing kitchen layout. These include measurements for the work triangle—the distances between the three primary work spaces (cooking surface, sink, and refrigerator). If you follow these guidelines, you should have a kitchen that is comfortable to use.

Another important thing to consider is the space between an island and the opposite countertop. You want a minimum distance of 36 inches, but 42 inches is better. I have seen many kitchens with less than 30 inches, and this is too narrow. And, it's always better to keep as much distance as possible between cold appliances and heat-producing appliances.

Some contractors provide kitchen design as part of their services. A good kitchen designer is very important. Work closely with them so you get the best possible results from this big investment.

Lora's Replay

The home I grew up in, which was built in the 1960s, had a big kitchen, but the refrigerator was positioned by itself in a corner and between two doorways. Every time we got something from the refrigerator, we had to walk to the other side of the room to put it on the counter. We went back and forth several times if we were getting a lot or removing things in the front to reach the back. It was a terrible layout and so annoying. You always need a landing area near the refrigerator!

Robert's Rule #23

Make sure the refrigerator has a countertop within reach, on the side of the door opening. With a double door refrigerator, a shelf is good on either side. It's also great to have an island in front of the refrigerator.

KITCHEN STYLE AND CABINET DOORS

The style of cabinet door you pick should fit with the overall style you've chosen for the kitchen. Some door styles are more universal than others. For example, a Shaker door can work for a contemporary kitchen or a country farmhouse look.

There are many different kitchen styles to choose from, and chances are, you've already seen some that you like—maybe in a magazine, a big box store, or even in a friend's kitchen.

Kitchen Styles

Following is a list of some of the most popular kitchen styles, including a brief description, from HGTV.com[1]:

Cottage — Cozy, comfortable, vintage features. Lots of color, painted cabinets, rustic or salvaged flooring, playful patterned fabrics.

Traditional — Still the reigning design style. The timeless look of traditional kitchens speaks to most of us. Classic elements without looking too stodgy or trapped in a time warp. Painted or stained-glass doors with traditional mullion doors. Standard traditional crown and trim.

Transitional — This style blends the best of traditional familiarity with modern sophistication to create comfortable, livable spaces.

Old World — Intricate moldings, hand-carved details, and dark woods are hallmarks of this European-influenced style.

Modern — This style is cousin to Contemporary; streamlined and sophisticated with unadorned doors, chrome hardware, and flush settings. Add straight lines and a matte finish for the Modern look.

Contemporary — Sleek, custom flush cabinets, minimalist doors on wall cabinets, oversized chrome pulls on lower cabinet doors.

Romantic — White or richly stained cabinets adorned with ornamental molding. Romantic style is reminiscent of Old World style that includes ornate moldings, furniture-like cabinets, and European accents, but adds a decidedly feminine feel.

Craftsman — Simple Shaker-style cabinet door details, open shelves, floating shelves, farmhouse sink.

---

1. "Top Kitchen Design Styles," HGTV.com, accessed June 2018, https://www.hgtv.com/remodel/kitchen-remodel/top-kitchen-design-styles.

Tuscan — Sun-warmed tones, often featuring elements that are seen in both traditional and Southwestern design. Copper and handmade tiles and subtly distressed stone or wood floors are often a feature.

Southwest — This design type is influenced by Native American, Mexican, and Spanish heritage with some design elements from Puebla Revival and Spanish Mission/Spanish Colonial. Large exposed timbers, stucco walls, brick or flagstone floors. May include some ironwork and colorful ceramic tile. Rustic-looking cabinets.

Rustic Industrial — This is a look that resembles an 1800s or early 1900s manufacturing facility. Rustic wood floors and beams, explosion proof lighting, industrial style chairs. Cabinets could be a rustic wood with some metal brackets or even metal cabinetry.

Mid-Century — This style is all about flat-paneled cabinets, light-colored walls, and pastel design accents. Appliances had rounded corners and shiny handles. Most new kitchens have only a touch of mid-century.

Coastal — Light colors in soft hues, accessories and artwork that reminds you of life by the water. Cabinet styles, woods, and colors can vary with this design type.

Cabinet Doors

There are quite a few different door style selections available. A few of the most common are described below. Our most popular door is a raised panel mitered door.

Cope and Stick — This door style looks like a tongue-and-groove joint and has a square look when complete. This style is less expensive to make than a mitered door.

Miter — This door style is connected on a 45-degree angle at each corner and is a more elegant and expensive door.

Flat Panel — This refers to the center part of the door and indicates that it does not have a raised panel in the middle. A Shaker door has a flat panel.

Raised Panel — This refers to the center part of the cabinet door that has a raised section, referred to as panel raise.

Inset Doors — This cabinet door sits inside the face frame and has an exposed hinge, unlike most cabinet doors that sit on the face frame and have an overlay.

Sweet Spot

More and more, we are installing a rustic industrial look with floating wood shelves in kitchens, providing a beautiful contrast with the cabinets.

Sweet Spot

Brushed brass, antique brushed brass, and antique gold hardware and fixtures are popular favorites at this publishing.

CABINET MATERIALS

Selecting your cabinets is something that usually needs to happen early in the process. You start by picking a wood species. The most common wood used for cabinets today is maple. It has a smooth grain that looks good either painted or stained. Other common woods are poplar, cherry, oak, and birch. Less common are hickory, ash, and mahogany.

Medium Density Fiberboard (MDF) can be a lower-cost option for cabinets. Many cabinet boxes are made out of this, as well as some cabinet doors and drawer fronts. Some doors use this as a core with a real-wood veneer over it. A veneer is a thin slice of wood—approximately 1/8 inch thick—that is glued to a core panel creating the look of a solid wood cabinet. It comes in almost every species of wood, such as maple, cherry, hickory, etc.

Other solid-wood alternatives include Rigid Thermofoil (RTF) and Thermally Fused Laminate (TFL) technologies where the MDF core has a plastic foil heat-shrunk over the door or a thicker laminate fused to it.

The advantage of MDF is that it's inexpensive. However, that cost savings comes with some disadvantages as well. MDF can swell if it gets wet or is exposed to too much moisture. It is hard to repair and is very dense and heavy, so it doesn't look very good stained.

We don't think it's the best choice for areas like kitchens and baths, which are exposed to a lot of moisture and steam. The plastic and laminate versions can change color over time, and the edges can curl up if exposed to oven heat. The technology has improved, and newer doors are better than the original ones from the 90s. There are some applications where they work very well. So, if you're trying to save some money, these could be an option.

CABINET BOXES

The cabinet box provides the structure and support for your cabinet. Until about the early 1980s, these were always made out of real plywood. After that, MDF and particle board boxes became popular and are still used on most production cabinets today. MDF is actually fine for these (unless they get wet which makes them crumble and fall apart). If you are having new cabinets built, I would recommend an all plywood box. When our company builds custom cabinets, we always use an all plywood box. It is stronger, more durable, and lasts longer than MDF.

Framed Cabinets

The most common type of cabinet construction in the US is what we refer to as a framed cabinet. The doors are mounted to a face frame, which is usually made of a hard wood. Behind this face frame is the cabinet box.

We create a face frame out of 1" x 2"s or something similar in size. There are vertical pieces called stiles, and horizontal pieces called rails. This is by far the strongest cabinet design because it allows you to build a plywood box and attach a rigid face frame, making it very strong and durable. The door is mounted to this face frame.

You may be asked what kind of overlay you want. The overlay is the amount of distance the door overlaps the face frame. The overlay with the newer hidden hinges usually ranges from ½ to 1 ½ inches. The larger overlay gives you a look called full overlay. This is where you see a minimum amount of face frame. This is also called a European style look, which can be a little confusing because most European cabinets are what we refer to as frameless. Another, but less common, option is an inset door, which actually sits within the face frame.

European Frameless Cabinets

European frameless refers to cabinets without a face frame that have a full overlay door. This means that when you look at the cabinets, you see very little of anything but the doors and drawer fronts. Many frameless cabinets are not very structurally sound. As a result, it's not uncommon to see the bottom of the cabinet hanging down below the doors. A framed cabinet is much sturdier. You can still have a full overlay door with a framed cabinet. We do make custom-built frameless cabinets which are very strong because we make them out of strong plywood and attach them better than most production frameless cabinets.

Drawer Boxes

Like cabinets, drawer boxes can be built out of many different materials. Nicer cabinets will have dovetailed, clear-coated boxes made of maple or birch. Less expensive cabinets will have MDF drawer boxes. Usually, these will also have the cheaper nylon drawer slides, while the solid wood boxes will have heavy-duty full extension glides. For both our custom cabinet and refacing projects, we generally use birch dovetailed with 5/8-inch sides and a plywood bottom. If the drawer is for pots and pans, we will use a half-inch thick bottom to give it more strength.

Many kitchens built before the 1970s will have old plywood drawer boxes with a center overhead track and a roller under each drawer. These are very wobbly and almost impossible to adjust. You will notice this when you are trying to retrieve something from the back of the drawer and about four inches of the drawer is still in the cabinet. We always use full extension glides. Full extension means that the glide brings the drawer box to the edge of the face frame, exposing the entire drawer for easy access of the entire content space.

Side-mount and undermount glides are newer and are the most popular. Side-mounted require about a half-inch clearance on each side of the drawer box to the side of the cabinet frame. This allows room for the glide to attach to the drawer box and to the side of the face frame. If you have old glides and have at least a half-inch clearance on each side, then it is a quick fix to change them to an updated glide! In all of our new drawer boxes, we use undermount drawer glides. This makes the drawer box a little wider, and it hides the glides making it look nicer when the drawer box is open. And it is very sturdy.

Cushion-Close Drawer Boxes

Over the past 10 years or so, the cabinet industry has moved toward the soft-close or cushion-close feature on drawers. I am not a big fan of this device in all situations because of the way they function. Most are designed to operate by the user pulling the drawer open against tension, which is actually cocking a trigger. When you push the drawer closed it catches on this trigger and allows the soft-close function to operate.

The problem with this is that the tension can be difficult for some people (like the elderly or someone with arthritis) and makes it hard for them to use the drawers. For this type of client, I prefer the full-extension, heavy-duty glides without the soft-close function. A few manufacturers are beginning to come out with models that minimize this tension effect. Because most of our clients ask for them, we have gone to the soft-close as standard on all of our projects. But I do ask who will be using the kitchen and prefer the non-soft-close in the situations mentioned above.

Robert's Rule #24

Before choosing soft-close drawer glides, consider who will be using them. If an elderly person or someone with arthritis will be using them, you may want to reconsider. Since the mechanism works by "cocking a trigger" when the drawer is first opened, it may be difficult for some because it requires extra resistance.

Soft-Close Doors

There are several types of soft-close door hinges available, and these do not have the same problem as the drawers. They tend to have a cylinder that opens by itself that allows it to slowly catch the door in the last inch of travel. The only caveat I have here is that you may get used to slamming the cabinet doors at your house because the mechanism will catch and slow the door. Then, when you go to the neighbor's house and do the same thing, it will be very loud (and could even cause a crack).

There is also a separate attachment that can give you the same effect. It screws to the face frame and catches the door, allowing it to soft-close. If you have regular hinges that are still working correctly, and you want the soft-close function on the doors, this is an easy solution.

Glass Doors

There are two types of glass cabinet doors—doors with mullions and those without. Mullions are the wood divider bars that create the true divided light look. The mullion door is very traditional looking. A glass door without mullions looks a little more European.

Glass choice can also change the look of the cabinet. You can choose traditional clear glass, colored glass, or decorative glass. Clear glass allows you to easily see items within the cabinet. Seeded glass has little bubbles, which is harder to see through and gives the appearance of old-time hand-blown glass. There are quite a few different types of decorative glass available. The website, AIGlass.com, has a nice selection of specialty glass.

If you want to install a light in the top of a cabinet to shine down on the items displayed, then you want to choose glass shelves instead of wood to allow the light to flow through and not be obstructed in the lower shelves.

Robert's Replay

I had a client who had nine-foot ceilings, and her cabinets were 42-inches high on the wall, leaving 12 inches above. She wanted to add cabinets with glass doors and lights above her existing cabinets, so she could display her decorative pottery. We used Shaker-style doors and LED lights. We also installed a farmhouse sink and some bead board on the back of the peninsula. We added light rail molding, under-cabinet LED lights, and topped it off with white granite countertops. The transformation was amazing!

FINISHES

There are two main finish choices—painted and stained. Each one has quite a few options. You can also choose accent glazes and specialty finishes, like distressed. Most of the time, if you pick dark colors, it's better to go with a stain, not paint. Dark paint colors tend to show marks more easily.

Distressed doors look like they have been around for a long time and have been used heavily. This is accomplished by roughing up the edges and random spots on the door to replicate an old door, and it can be done in combination with antiquing. Some people like to mark them up with nails and other items.

> **Stains** — There are several types of stain finishes available. The more common ones today include wipe-on stains with a lacquer finish, lacquer toners, and conversion varnishes. There are both oil- and water-based products.
>
> In our shop, we prefer to do things the old-fashioned way by using wiping stains that penetrate into the wood. We go over that with sanding sealer and then clear lacquer. We have very few callbacks on our work. Another reason we use this process is that we are frequently asked to repair different finishes, and we've found that our process performs better than most.

Paints — The most commonly used paints for cabinets are latex, oil-based, and pigmented lacquer. Each has different characteristics as well as pros and cons. We prefer to use oil-based or lacquer for kitchens and baths. These areas experience changes in temperature and high levels of moisture. We also have very few callbacks using these products.

Sweet Spot — Contrasting Colors

Contrasting colors are a new trend. Homeowners are contrasting the color on the island and/or perimeter base cabinets from the wall cabinets. Shades of gray or navy are the new popular colors, yet white shades will always remain a classic.

CABINET TRIM

The look of cabinets can be enhanced by adding trim. There are many types of wood trims available to add the details you see in a kitchen. Here are several popular types:

Crown Molding — This is molding that attaches to the top of the cabinet or at the top of a wall, where the cabinet connects to the ceiling. Crown molding comes in many different types and sizes, including traditional crown, Shaker crown, and inset crown.

Inset crown is designed to have another piece of molding attached to it to give it a distinct look. Some examples would be dentil mold, rope mold, or egg and dart, to name a few. Each one comes in various sizes to achieve the desired look.

Crown molding can be made up of single or multiple pieces with each additional molding creating a more dynamic look. A two-piece crown can be a piece of standard base molding turned upside down with crown molding attached to it on the bottom and the top of the crown attached to the ceiling. A three-piece crown could have the same thing but add a piece of base molding on the ceiling as well. Another common practice is to drop down about six inches and add a base cap trim below the crown, then paint from the base cap to the crown molding in the trim color to give the illusion that it is a larger piece of crown.

Light Rail — This trim is designed to attach at the bottom of the wall cabinet. It helps hide the under-cabinet lighting and also dresses up the bottom of the cabinet. This can be inset as well, allowing for some rope mold trim or egg and dart to be attached to it to give it a more dramatic look.

Toe Kick Trim — This is trim that attaches around the toe kick area at the floor. It could be a piece of decorative base molding. It could also be a trim molding or decorative feet that make the cabinet look like a piece of furniture.

Fluted Fillers — Most kitchens have some areas that are a few inches wide and are too narrow for a cabinet. These gaps need to be filled and can be more decorative by adding fillers with flutes on them. A fluted filler looks like a flat board with multiple, vertical grooves cut in it. Fillers are typically placed between the wall and the edge of a cabinet or between two cabinets, but they can also be added at the end of a cabinet. These can be used on both base and wall cabinets.

Applied Moldings — These can be used to create a decorative panel on the sides of the cabinets or the back of the island or peninsula. There are several types of molding that can be used to come up with different looks. They dress up a plain cabinet and are inexpensive for the value they give.

Blind Corners — This is where two cabinets come together with one cabinet reaching all the way to the corner, creating mostly inaccessible space. Some builders stop the cabinets and don't give you access to this area. I don't recommend that!

If the design allows, you can often access these cabinets from the opposite side, for example from the back of a peninsula. There are also a few ways to access this space utilizing pull-out shelves. There are some pantry-type cabinets that use this space well. They consist of a fold-out storage unit on the inside of the door and some pull-out shelves.

ACCESSORIES

As you begin to finalize the plan details for your new kitchen space, there are a few "extras" you may want to consider. These are things that can make a kitchen more functional.

Let's start with the trash. A door-mounted, pull-out trash bin is almost required in today's kitchen. It is usually best located near the sink and prep area. It can be large enough to have two bins. The door-mounted option is preferred over the more basic "open the door and reach in to pull out the can" version. They come in various sizes and options, so you can match it up to your cabinet opening. It usually takes a cabinet that is 15- or 18-inches wide, because after you subtract the frames on a 15-inch cabinet you end up with 11 to 12 inches of usable width, which is about the size of the pull-out trash unit that has to fit in this space.

Sweet Spot — Trashcan Pull-Out

> A trashcan pull-out, a "must have" now, is a door-mounted trashcan pull-out cabinet. Just pull it open and wipe waste into it right from the countertop! It can even have a shelf at the back to store your trash bags. A 35-quart trashcan fits in a cabinet with a drawer above it and a 50-quart fits a full-height door. I suggest a cabinet that is about the width of the can since the extra space beside it gets unused. Really, how many things in your kitchen are you willing to store next to the trash?

Sweet Spot — Built-in Cutting Board with Trashcan Pull-Out

> This is a very cool design feature. From the outside, the cutting board looks like a drawer. But, pull it out, and there is a hole where scraps can go right into the trash below! This is a popular "must have" variation, taking care of two things in one place.

Pull-out cabinet shelves are also a great feature and are sometimes more useful than drawers. You can actually get more in them than in a stack of drawers because you eliminate the drawer-glide rail and the space the drawer boxes take up.

Pull-out shelves come in just about every size. We custom build ours for the particular layout. I like to use them for storing things like plastic containers and especially for pots and pans.

When we do refacing projects and come across a location that has two doors with a stile between (stiles are the vertical cabinet face dividers), we will often remove the stile, which allows us to put a wider pull-out drawer in the space.

Pull-outs in a deep pantry eliminate the problem of having items stacked, making it difficult to know what you have. We usually build our pull-outs out of birch, dovetailed with clear coat, and a half moon cutout at the front. We use full-extension, heavy-duty glides for strength and ease of motion.

Sweet Spot — Pot and Pan Pull-Out

Big pots and pans need a sturdy shelf. Ours are custom made, and we upgrade the standard materials with heavy-duty bottoms and heavy-duty drawer glides. One of the best decisions you can make is to have pot/pan pull-out shelves installed. The pot/pan three-drawer base is another option, but you get a little less space. You absolutely need one or the other!

Sweet Spot — Vertical Tray Cabinets

These are a good way to make use of a narrow space (about 10 inches or less). This cabinet is great for storing something every kitchen has—cutting boards, trays, cookie sheets, flat pans, etc.

Sweet Spot — Pull-out Spice Racks

These are popular on each side of the range. They are great organizers and are accessible from both sides. A small basket or two can be added to this rack, which is perfect for measuring spoons and small measuring cups. A narrow space of around five to seven inches is all you need for this cabinet.

Sweet Spot — Coffee Station

A separate coffee/tea station has become increasingly popular. Some have a pull-out shelf while others are free standing. They usually have doors to keep supplies hidden when not in use. This has also become a popular place to store hospitality refreshments.

Robert's Replay

We had a client with a stuffed and disorganized pantry closet. He wanted a wine cooler and rack. We took the shelves out of this closet and added a wine cooler, a granite countertop, and a wine rack with a wall cabinet and under-cabinet lighting on a separate switch. We installed French doors to close it in, and the transformation was astounding! The added view through the French doors became a popular focal point.

A common problem I see is a damaged sink base bottom. This is the cabinet floor area under your sink. Sometimes, the sink drain leaks. Usually, people stuff this area full of cleaning supplies and miscellaneous items. It's easy to bump a drain line taking things in and out, causing it to leak a little. After a while, the leaking causes the floor of the cabinet to swell and discolor. One way to prevent this is to use a sink base drip tray. This is a plastic tray designed to fit under the plumbing in a standard sink base cabinet. If you get a leak, the tray will collect the water and protect the cabinet until you notice it and get it fixed. Of course, this won't help with a major leak, like a supply line leak, but it will protect your cabinet base from drips and spills!

CABINET HARDWARE

Knobs and pulls are the finishing touches for new cabinets. They can help the kitchen make a statement. They can push it more contemporary or keep it very traditional. You can go with knobs on doors and pulls on the drawers, or all knobs or all pulls. There is no right or wrong way to do it. I prefer to match the finish of the hardware with the finish of the sink faucet, but you don't HAVE to do this, I just think it goes together better. You can get hardware in a variety of finishes. Currently in the South, brushed nickel and oil-rubbed bronze are most common, although others are gaining popularity.

Robert's Rule #25

When choosing hardware, try to avoid a knob that is square or straight lined. They will constantly be turning out of level or plumb and will bother you every time you see them.

Robert's Rule #26

When selecting drawer pulls, beware of pulls that stick out on each side. They can catch clothing and stretch or tear it!

KITCHEN FIXTURES

Just as there are many cabinet types, materials, and styles, there are also lots of sinks and faucets to choose from. Some of the more common selections are described below.

Note: You need to have your sink and faucet picked out before your countertop is cut and installed since the size, number, and placement of hole cut-outs depends upon what you pick.

- **Farmhouse sinks** — These are identified by the fact that you can see the front of the sink. They are quite popular and can be stainless steel, brass, porcelain, or composite. When modifying a cabinet base for a farmhouse sink we have to make vertically shorter doors and build extra support in the bottom of the cabinet for the sink to sit on. These are also called apron front sinks.
- **Copper sinks** — These give a country/rustic look similar to the farmhouse sink. They are available either as an apron front sink or for undermount

placement and come in a hammered copper finish or antique-looking patina.

Vegetable sinks — This sink is great for washing vegetables, fruit, lettuce, draining noodles, etc. It's smaller than a standard sink (around 12 inches wide) and is ideally placed at your prep area, preferably to one side so you have plenty of counter space beside it to prepare your meal.

70/30 split sinks — If you do not have space for a separate vegetable sink, the 70/30 sink is a great alternative. It has a small veggie sink on one side and an extra-large sink on the other. If possible, place the cleaning side on the same side as the dishwasher and it will be easy to keep the dirty dish mess away from the food.

Sweet Spot — Vegetable Sink

This keeps your food preparation area separate from your clean-up area. How great is that? It is also a perfect location for ice when you are entertaining because it has a built-in drain.

Note: If you like to entertain, make handling a crowd part of your design when finalizing your kitchen layout. If you have a big group over and want to keep it casual, you want to have enough counter space so that everyone can streamline through your prepared dishes in buffet style and fix plates. An island works great in this capacity, too. If you're adding a separate vegetable sink, this is a good reason to have it placed on one side of your primary counter to allow more continuous space for food placement.

Pot Filler faucets — Popular for look and efficiency, this mounts behind the range, swinging out when you need it. It is also good for large bulky things, like plants and humidifiers, that are hard to fit under a regular sink faucet. A faucet with two valves can minimize the possibility of a leak.

Gooseneck faucets — This raised faucet allows for so much more room you will not know how you ever cleaned large things without it! There are many types of gooseneck faucets, and some of them are very sophisticated. Some have a pull-down feature and may have a spray wand that's great for washing veggies and cleaning. They are costlier than a faucet with a side sprayer, but side sprayers do have a more vintage look, if that's what you are going for.

Sweet Spot

A sense of warmth is added to the kitchen with the fresh look of light-colored brick—either as a backsplash, encased in the cooktop setting, or as a cased opening between the kitchen and dining areas.

PANTRY

There are two kinds of pantries—a cabinet pantry and a drywall pantry. Most of the drywall pantries are about two to three feet wide and 24 inches deep. The cabinet pantries vary from about 18 to 36 inches wide.

If you have a space that is 24 inches deep, it will work great as your pantry, but you MUST have pull-out or swing-out shelves added so you can reach everything in the back effectively. The problem with a 24-inch-deep pantry without pull-out shelves is you're not able to access or see items in the back without removing a lot of things.

Robert's Replay

We were contracted by a client to remodel her laundry room and garage entry to accommodate a larger pantry. Her existing pantry was about the size of a small coat closet (30 inches wide by 24 inches deep) with about six ventilated pantry shelves.

She was going to be out of town the day we started, and she said she would have her daughter clean out the pantry.

When we got there that morning, it had not been emptied. You can probably imagine what it looked like, stuffed from floor to ceiling with cans, boxes, bags, and bottles. We spent over an hour removing the contents of this pantry. I noticed the dates on some of the items were at least 5 years old—likely there because they were stuck in the back and had not been seen in years. Thankfully, we built her a pantry that was 4 feet wide and 12 feet deep. It had plenty of shelving so accessing anything should no longer be a problem. This is the kind of issue that pull-out shelves in a pantry cabinet can eliminate.

OUTDOOR KITCHENS

This trend became especially popular during the most recent economic downturn. People were staying home more, and an outdoor kitchen provided a small getaway. Many of these spaces are covered for cooking, eating, TV watching, and/or fireplace relaxing. They are a great spot for entertaining.

The cabinets are usually made from metal or some type of wood that holds up well in an outdoor environment, like cedar, teak, and ipe woods. Cabinet boxes can be made from marine plywood. An outdoor kitchen is not usually large, but you can include some of the same amenities that are in your main kitchen, like an oven or pull-out shelves and trash bin, for example. Most of the time the cabinets are nestled in stone or brick with a natural stone top.

> *Sweet Spot* — Outdoor Grill Station
>
> If you're like me, you'd much rather keep the mess outside! Outdoor grill stations can be simple, or you may prefer a more elaborate setup for entertaining. They are all great. Ours is a rustic industrial look. It's mounted on a wall on our deck with wide beams on each side that are stained to look old, and I've added hooks where I hang grilling tools. The width is a bit more than the grill itself. We used corrugated metal for the overhang and the back wall and added two industrial-type light fixtures on each side with a matching outdoor switch and outlet. There is much outdoor innovation to consider if you prefer a more elaborate set-up.

GENERAL PROJECT CONSIDERATIONS

> **Floor protection** — Make sure whoever is working in your house does not tape paper or plastic directly to your hardwood flooring. Depending on the type and condition of the clear coat finish, the tape can pull it right up. Even the lightest adhesive tape can do this. After you pull up

the finish, the only option is to buff and re-apply a new top coat finish. Have them tape it to the base boards, shoe molding, or cabinets (not freshly painted!), but NOT the hardwood floor!

Moving refrigerators — Take great caution when moving refrigerators, as you can easily damage the hardwoods. It's best to put cardboard or hardboard down first before rolling it forward. Another thing to keep in mind is the ice maker line. If you have a copper line, they are bad to kink and will start leaking after you push it back toward the wall. If it starts leaking, you may not know it!

Sweet Spot — Utility Closet

If you don't have a utility room but DO have a small closet, you'd be surprised how easily you can organize your cleaning supplies. Save floor space for the vacuum cleaner, mop bucket, and other big things. Hang a fabric shoe bin on the inside of the door and store your cleaning products in each section. You can also add a larger shoe organizer from a hanging rod to fit paper towels/cloths and larger supplies. With everything in eyesight, it's easy to just grab and go!

Sweet Spot — Mounted Garment Drying Rack

This is a convenient laundry room space saver. The rack folds into the wall when not needed but can be pulled out to air dry clothes.

Sweet Spot — Separate Tool Boxes!

We've found that it's best if a husband and wife each have their own tool box. They tend to contain different types of tools, and you don't have to worry about not being able to find things that were "borrowed."

Lora's Replay

One of my daughters used her husband's nice paint brush for a project and forgot to rinse it afterwards because she had to do something with a child. This happened twice. He got upset, and she just couldn't see the deal with a paintbrush. I told her a man considers his nice paint brush as one of his tools, and she needed her own. She had not thought of it like that. Now, she has her own tool box with her own paintbrush that she can use the way she wants.

CHAPTER 5

BATHROOMS

Bathrooms are usually the second most important spaces in a home when it comes to home value. When someone is buying a new home, both the kitchen and master bath play a huge role in their decision about a house.

Other bathrooms in the house are important as well. For example, the powder room is usually on the main floor and is the bathroom guests are most likely to visit. The hall bathrooms or Jack and Jill baths are usually closer to family bedroom areas and are typically the baths for the children.

A buyer with children may not be as picky about these areas as they are about the master bath, but, at some point, these bathrooms will need to be updated as well. Say goodbye to that pink tile and tub, or something even worse! I have seen several chocolate-brown bathtubs with matching sink and toilet. If you have one of these, you need to get it updated NOW!

Robert's Replay

I don't always recommend updating a bath. I was in a house recently in Atlanta that was built in 1941. The owner showed me the powder room on the main floor, which was pink. She thought they should rip it out and update it before they sold the house. I looked at it and saw that it was original to the house and in excellent condition. The floor had beautiful mosaic tile and the walls had a tile wainscoting with a beautiful accent. The only thing it needed was an updated sink. Someone had put in a small, cheap vanity and sink in the 1970s. I recommended a retro sink that hangs on the wall and has metal legs—a style that would fit the room perfectly.

> **Robert's Rule #27**
>
> If the house is old and you have a bathroom that is original, your best option may be to restore it back to its original glory instead of tearing it out and doing a complete update.

MASTER BATH

In some homes, especially those built in the 1970s and 1980s, the house has a lot of floor space, but the rooms are cut up and the baths and closets are small. Homes with this type of floor plan can potentially increase both bathroom and closet size by simply moving walls around.

Robert's Replay

We did a project for the son of a past Georgia Tech football coach. His family was growing, and they needed a bigger house with a bigger yard. They chose a house built in the early 1980s that had lots of room but was a typical house from that era. The master bedroom was a good size, but the master bath and closet were very small.

We came in, analyzed the space, and concluded that if we lost one of the four bedrooms on the second floor, we could expand the master suite. There was plenty of room in the basement to create a bedroom, so they didn't have to completely lose one. The master bath backed up to another bedroom. By bumping into this room, we were able to enlarge the master closet and the master bath, creating enough space for a big walk-in closet (complete with a closet organizing system) as well as a master bath with a large walk-in shower and a separate tub. This totally changed the look and feel of the master bedroom, resulting in a true "master suite."

In another house, we didn't have quite as much space, so we couldn't build a big master bath. But, we were able to use part of the closet in the next bedroom to create enough room to allow us to put in a shower along with a soaking tub. Be creative when it comes to using the space that you have. Sometimes just a few small changes can make a huge difference!

THINGS TO CONSIDER IN A NEW BATHROOM

There are many decisions that need to be made before starting your bath project. From tile to fixtures to shower or tub, you'll need to have a pretty good idea of what you want before the remodel begins.

The following are some things you'll want to take into consideration when planning your new bathroom.

Tile floor — You may have your heart set on a certain type of tile you saw. While almost anything can be accommodated if you have the funds to pay for it, you will need to find out if the existing floor system can support the material you want to use. It may need to be reinforced before using a heavy tile or natural stone. (Without appropriate support, the floor might not cave in, but it may flex enough to cause the grout to crack).

You'll also need to give some thought to the tile design you want to use. Do you want a square pattern, diagonal, etc.? More complicated patterns tend to have more waste, so you end up paying for materials that will end up as scraps.

Do you want to install a heated floor system under the tile? If so, where do you want the heat mat to be located and how sophisticated do you want the controls to be?

Do you want to use cut tile to create a tile base or just use a standard wood base?

Robert's Rule #28

Always use a cement backer board under your tile when setting on a wood floor system. This will help provide a stronger tile floor and will help prevent cracks and loose tiles due to poor adhesion.

If the floor is not level, you might want to stay away from large tiles (like 16" x 16" or larger). Smaller tiles are more forgiving of floor inconsistencies. Large tiles can make the unevenness more apparent, with one end of the tile sticking up higher than the other. Depending on the severity of the problem, sometimes a floor leveling compound can be used to fix this.

Tile shower — Do you want a full-tile shower? And, similar to the tile floor questions, you'll want to do some research to decide what look you want for your shower and whether the existing structure is sufficient to support the weight the new tile adds (if not, you'll likely incur some additional expense to reinforce).

An important part of the planning process is to find out if your contractor is qualified to do the tile work or if it should it be subbed out to a specialist. Many contractors do not know how to install a true mud-set vinyl liner tile shower floor.

Ask your installer how he installs his shower pans. If he never mentions the word "pre-bed," then I wouldn't use him. If your installer neglects to place a pre-bed under the vinyl liner, then it can create a dam of about a ½ inch where water will just sit forever. This can cause several problems.

Robert's Rule #29

When installing a mud-set pan over vinyl liner in a tile shower floor, be sure your installer knows how to install a pre-bed under the vinyl liner.

When we install a new shower, we always recommend changing out the shower valve, trim, and showerhead at the same time. These can develop leaks over time, and it is easier to change them out after the old tile is off the wall than later, when you have little or no access to the plumbing.

A nice addition when installing new plumbing is to add a separate, handheld shower wand. This provides flexibility for special bathing circumstances, for example when recovering from surgery or bathing the elderly. It also comes in handy for cleaning the shower and bathing the dog!

Sweet Spot — Add Custom Temperature Controls

Heated towel racks and heated floors provide winter warmth, and a ceiling fan keeps you cool while dressing in the warm weather months. These are great additions to master baths and can have programmable thermostats for easy comfort.

Towel Hooks — These are sometimes overlooked, but we think you'll be glad you have them. We have something we call the "Fran hook." This is named after a client who asked me where people hang their wet wash cloths. She didn't like the idea of laying them across the top of the shower valve or over the door. We installed a stud in the wall of the shower that we could tile around with screws sticking out. When we were done, we installed two stainless steel hooks. It was the perfect solution, and it was very attractive!

Mirrors — When remodeling a bathroom, you have to decide what to do with the mirror. One option is to select a plate glass mirror and use a product to wrap the edge of the mirror with a frame. We use a product called Mirror Mate, which comes in a variety of designs and colors. This can be less expensive than finding a full decorative hanging mirror. It also solves the problem if you want a larger mirror or two mirrors in the same room that are different sizes.

Shower Enclosures — What type of shower enclosure do you want? Shower enclosures come in various designs. Frameless enclosures look just like they sound—they have almost no framing and are attached to the wall with clips. This is the most expensive type of enclosure. It is custom made and can be almost any size. There are many options. The glass can be clear, frosted, or coated. The fittings can come in many different finishes, such as brushed nickel, chrome, oil rubbed bronze, and several others.

A lower cost option is a framed enclosure. These have frames at the top and on the sides to support the glass. These also come in several colors and finishes.

Bathroom Exhaust Fans — Depending on the age of your home, you may not have an exhaust fan. The old code maintained that if you had a window in the toilet area, you didn't need to have an exhaust fan. I guess somebody realized that if it's cold outside, you won't open the window! The code has been changed to require a fan even if you have a window. And, most codes now require a separate exhaust fan in the bath area to help remove moisture there.

Robert's Rule #30

When installing an exhaust fan in a bathroom, it's usually a good idea to wire it so it turns on with the bathroom light or, in a larger bathroom, have it come on with the shower light.

There are many types of exhaust fans. You can get just a basic fan, a fan with a light, or even one that includes a heater. They come with different noise (quiet) levels and air-movement levels (measured as CFMs or cubic feet per minute).

Sometimes you might actually choose a louder fan. If you have a bathroom right off a main area where guests gather, and you really don't want to hear what's going on in the bathroom, get a loud fan. Also, you might want fan sound to sleep at night. If so, make sure you can hear it. Sometimes quiet is not best! A bath fan can provide a smooth, calming sound for sleeping children.

Robert's Replay

A few years ago, I was called out to a home in Atlanta that was probably built in the 1980s. The homeowner had lived there for quite a few years. He showed me his hall bath and said he was having some mold problems. When he showed me the bathroom, I couldn't believe my eyes. There was black mold growing on the ceiling and walls!

The room had no ventilation so moisture had built up and was causing mold to grow. This homeowner worked for the Centers for Disease Control and Prevention (CDC) and was well aware of the dangers of mold in a home. We recommended installing a good, strong exhaust fan and venting it to the outside. We also suggested tying the power into the switch for the bathroom light, so the fan comes on whenever the light is on. We have found that most people don't bother to turn the fan on if you keep it separate. The mold was treated, the room was painted, and the new fan system now keeps the moisture in check.

Sweet Spot — Grooming Organizer Drawer

Many of our clients want a place to keep their hair dryer, curling iron, straightening rod, etc. They want them to be accessible, but hidden. And they want an outlet in the drawer or on a shelf under the vanity sink so they can plug them in. It has to be a GFCI outlet, but this is a nice way to hide your cords and yet still provide for convenient use of appliances.

Sweet Spot — Makeup Lap Drawer

Many women appreciate the organization of a lap drawer, which has dividers to keep everything in order and off the vanity top. This is great for lotions, makeup, brushes, cleansers, and the small things we use constantly.

Sweet Spot — Fold-out Ironing Board

If an ironing board isn't near our clothes, many of us will just pick something different to wear. If your closet or bathroom has space for a fold-out ironing board, you should have one installed! It looks like a drawer when shut, but when opened, the drawer folds out to a full-sized board. Even if you keep a traditional ironing board in your laundry room for other family members to use, you will love having your own next to your dressing area.

Tubs and Showers

Jetted Garden Tubs — These were popular in the 1980s and 1990s. Today, most people prefer a soaking tub. The jetted tubs built in this era have a few problems. If the size of a tub is too big, the water heater doesn't have enough capacity to fill it. Keeping it clean is another problem. A bathtub doesn't have a filtering system to clean the water, so all the dirt and soap scum just collects in the jet areas. And, it's hard to get dirt and soap scum out of jets! Today, we have better designs on jetted tubs and tankless water heaters which make these more functional.

Freestanding Tub — We are seeing more people who want to remove their big soaking tub or jetted tub and install a freestanding tub. Some prefer the claw foot design. Others choose from the many, more contemporary styles, which have a base the tub sits in or are a one-piece design. We usually recommend tiling the floor beneath and up the walls to wainscoting height to protect from splashing.

Robert's Replay

I was looking at a bathroom with a client who had just purchased a home. It had a jetted garden tub. She was contemplating whether to keep the tub or replace it. I shared with her that some people didn't like these tubs because of their tendency to hold dirt and soap scum in the jets and in the piping behind the tub. As we talked about this, I reached over and hit the button to turn it on for a second. It blew the worst looking mess you have ever seen out of the jets, and she was just aghast! Needless to say, we changed out that tub.

Curb-less Showers — This refers to a barrier-free entry into the shower. A standard tile shower has what is referred to as a curb. This is just what it sounds like. It's usually about four to six inches tall and keeps the water in the shower from running into the other part of the bathroom. A newer, contemporary trend is to have a sleek, flat entry into the shower. Often, the bathroom floor flows seamlessly into the shower area.

While some people just like the minimalist design of a curb-less shower, others choose it for accessibility. If you have an older occupant or someone that has difficulty lifting their leg or maintaining balance, a curb-less system may be a great solution.

Obviously, some additional planning is required. The floor has to have enough slope so the water will run to the drain and not into other areas of the bathroom. Long, narrow linear drains are now available. These are placed at one end of the shower, away from the entrance (as opposed to the standard round drain placed in the center of a curbed shower). The floor is sloped gradually toward the back wall where the linear drain has been placed. This allows the water to hit the floor and run away from the entrance of the shower. Add a few grab bars, and you'll have an excellent shower for anyone!

Shower Niche — Include one! Every shower needs a place to put soap, shampoo, and other items. We install tiled shower niches into the wall to hold these items. A seat in the shower or a toe step-hold are also popular.

Robert's Replay

We were remodeling a hall bath in a house built in the 1950s. The existing floor joist system was not sufficient to support the new floor, so the first thing we had to do was remove the old system and install full-size joists and a new subfloor. My guys removed all of this and went to lunch.

Pets and Remodeling

Always lock up pets and keep them out of the way while remodeling. Cats are especially curious about what's going on.

The homeowner had two cats but said not to worry about them. She said that we would never see them because they were scaredy-cats. She was right; we never saw them. The guys got back from lunch, installed the subfloor and went home for the night. That night, I got a call from the homeowner asking if we had seen the gray cat. I called the guys, and they said no.

She soon called back after discovering that the cat was in the floor! The guys went back out that night to remove the plywood subfloor and retrieve the trapped cat.

Robert's Rule #31

Always keep your pets secured and out of the way during construction—for their safety and the workers'. Bonus: it keeps pet hair from getting stuck in fresh paint!

CHAPTER 6
CABINET REFACING EXPLORED

ABOUT REFACING

An option for updating a kitchen when you have a tight budget is to consider "refacing" the cabinets instead of completely replacing them. With cabinet refacing, you keep your existing cabinet boxes and put a new face over them, upgrading your kitchen without a complete tear out. There are several ways of accomplishing this.

Cabinet refacing began in the early 1970s. The most common method back then was to apply a plastic laminate to the face frame and sides of the cabinet. Then, doors were made of plywood panel and covered in plastic laminate to match the face frames.

Today, cabinet refacing has gotten much more sophisticated. As mentioned in the Kitchens chapter, you have the choice of inexpensive (and we believe inferior) products like painted MDF (Medium Density Fiberboard) and RTF (Rigid Thermofoil) doors and drawer fronts. This is where a plastic foil or sheet is wrapped over an MDF panel.

These can look like real wood or can be a painted surface but have some drawbacks. For example, the areas next to the oven can shrivel up when too much heat is released from the oven. Or, the areas around the dishwasher or sink can absorb moisture and cause the MDF to expand. This can make the plastic come loose and sometimes just pop off the door. I have also seen white kitchens that have turned yellow from heat and moisture. Or worse, some doors turned yellow and some stayed white!

The companies that use these products like them because they are easy to install and easy to sell because they're inexpensive. They can usually finish a kitchen in a day or two. There are a few situations where I will recommend this product, but not many.

One thing Detail Design and Remodeling does is custom cabinet refacing. We use real wood doors, such as maple or cherry, and 1/4-inch real wood veneers on the face and sides. For a painted look, we will sometimes paint the boxes on-site and not use a veneer. We often modify or add cabinets. If we change drawer boxes, we usually use dovetailed and clear-coated with full-extension glides. We will add pull-out shelves in some cabinets to make them more functional.

Our goal is to create a kitchen with great quality that is functional and beautiful in a more cost effective and less intrusive way than a complete tear out. When we are finished, it is difficult to tell it has been refaced! Our tag line is "We apply Old World craftsmanship to create your dream kitchen where friends and family gather." Our kitchens are crafted—not produced!

IS REFACING RIGHT FOR YOU?

When deciding how you might update your kitchen, there are a few things to consider to help determine if your kitchen qualifies for a refacing:

1. Do you like the layout? Even though we can make a few modifications, there is a point where it makes more sense to replace the existing cabinets with new ones. Basically, the more changes you make to the layout by modifying existing cabinets, the closer you get to justifying a full tear out. Most refacing projects we do might have a few cabinet changes, but overall will keep the basic layout.

2. Are the cabinet boxes in good shape? We rarely see cabinets that are too bad to reface, but it does happen.
3. Do you have existing granite tops or something similar and don't want to replace them? We see this quite a lot. There is no practical, safe way to remove countertops to install new cabinets and then re-set the existing tops. Refacing is your best option to update the look of your kitchen.

When you look at a kitchen cabinet, the part you see is the most important. The doors, drawer fronts, face frames, and any trim set the style and look of the kitchen. One benefit of a custom cabinet refacing project is the ability to create the exact look you want. You may have an old 1990s white Thermofoil kitchen, and you want to go to a nice traditional stained look. That is easy to do. Maybe you have nine-foot ceilings, and your cabinets only go to eight feet (which is very common), but you want yours to go to the ceiling. Again, that is easy.

Another good example of a situation where refacing can make a big difference is in an older kitchen that has an eight-foot ceiling and 30-inch doors on the wall cabinets with a 12-inch door above. We manufacture a door that covers both spaces so when you open the door you have access to both compartments. This gives the look of a newer cabinet without the cost and time of tearing it out and replacing it.

We have an enormous number of door style options, color options, and trim options—certainly more options than new production cabinets. We can do almost anything you have in mind.

Confession: Before we started offering cabinet refacing, I would only sell full tear outs and install all new cabinets. I thought cabinet refacing was a "cheap" option that compromised on quality. But, I started to realize that there were fine quality refacing products and methods which, in many cases, were better than most production cabinets available.

Some of the benefits of cabinet refacing versus a full tear out are:

- You don't lose the use of the kitchen for four to six weeks.
- You save up to 50 percent off the price of a full tear out.
- The demolition phase is quicker.
- You can keep your backsplash if you want.
- If you already have newer countertops, you don't lose those (it's very difficult to re-use tops).

Some of our kitchen projects combine cabinet refacing and cabinet refinishing (painting or staining existing cabinets).

I recently looked at a kitchen where the island was only a few years old, but the rest of the kitchen was about 20 years old with MDF doors that were looking pretty rough. We refaced the outer part of the kitchen and just painted the island. This obviously saved the client time and money.

CHAPTER 7
COUNTERTOPS

Selecting countertops is an important step in the kitchen remodeling process. You can upgrade the entire look of your kitchen space in a relatively inexpensive way by simply replacing your existing countertops.

Today's homeowners have quite a few options when it comes to the types and styles of countertops. Laminate tops, introduced by the Formica Company, were popular starting in the 1940s and are still used today. Now, there are many color choices and style selections in laminate—some that even look like real granite and have special edging. Laminate countertops are still the least expensive tops available, but some of the custom design options can make the price creep up.

COUNTERTOP OPTIONS

There are now many popular alternatives to laminate countertops. They come in a wide range of materials, styles, and prices.

> **Solid Surface** — After laminates, the next countertops to really come on the scene were developed by DuPont Chemical Company in 1963, called Corian. These counters are easy-to-clean, durable surfaces with a consistent color. There are several other companies now that make solid surface tops. Some solid surface drawbacks, though, include a tendency to crack or scorch if subjected to high heat, such as when a hot pan is placed on it.

Engineered Stone/Quartz — This was invented about 50 years ago by a company called Breton. These countertops are made by binding resins and pieces of stone or stone-like materials. It has the solidness of real stone but can be created in consistent patterns like the solid surface tops. However, these can be costly. Breton still holds the original patent which limits competition and keeps prices high.

Natural Stone — This option is timeless, traditional, and still very popular. The price has come down considerably over the past 20 years as its availability has increased. The look and characteristics of natural stone can vary quite a bit, depending on the type of stone you want so do some research before choosing it. We use the 3CM (which is 3 centimeters or about 1½ inches thick) for countertops because it is more rigid.

Natural stone is porous and more susceptible to staining, so it needs to be sealed. Stone prices vary quite a bit based on supply and demand. The more rare and wild the pattern (exotic), the more expensive it is. You can choose many different edging options to give your kitchen that special look. Currently, natural stone still has a higher perceived value and may help increase the value of your home.

Concrete — This is a new entry into the kitchen top family. Concrete is very trendy, solid, and has a very modern look. It is also very expensive. But, it does have the advantage that it can be formed into any shape since it is a poured product. Like natural stone, it is very porous and has to be sealed on a regular basis.

Stainless Steel — If you want the look of a professional kitchen, then stainless steel is it, and it's expensive. But remember, it is not as "stainless" as you would think. It can stain and corrode and requires a good bit of care and maintenance.

Wood Countertops — Wood tops have probably been around since the beginning of time. They are very beautiful but require a lot of maintenance. They are built to order so you have quite a few design options, and they are available in many different wood species, which changes the look of them drastically.

They can be finished using a variety of different techniques. Depending on how they're finished, they may be fairly heat resistant, but not as much as some of the other countertops available. There's also always a chance you can damage the finish. They are somewhat soft and can scratch, but they won't crack or break like a solid surface top. Many times, a wood top will be used only on the island to create a unique look in the kitchen. For example, a rougher wood can be installed to give a butcher block look, or a more finished flat piece can create a furniture top look.

Reclaimed Wood — Another growing trend is the use of reclaimed wood for a countertop (usually for the island). This is wood that comes from an old building that has been torn down, and the wood was saved and repurposed. It's not unusual for this wood to be over 100 years old. It has a character of its own. We have some friends that own a company where they specialize in this. They tear down the old structure, kiln-dry the wood, and make furniture—like kitchen tables or conference room tables. Their work is amazing, and you can find them at SonsOfSawdust.com.

CHAPTER 8
ADDITIONS/GENERAL REMODELING

SHOULD YOU REMODEL?

I'm asked from time to time if I think it is better to add an addition to a house or do a major remodel, like a kitchen or bath. Or, is it better to just sell and buy a new house?

There are several factors to consider when answering those questions. With real estate, the first is always the same: Location! Location! Location! Is your home in an ideal location? Is it in a growing area with good schools? Is it close to your work? If it has these things going for it, then I would recommend staying put and remodeling that home.

Even if you choose to relocate, you may want to do some remodeling to improve the home you're trying to sell. A house that is outdated because it hasn't been renovated in a long time (or ever!) may be harder to sell. Or, you might have to sell at a lower price because the buyer knows they'll have to spend money to update everything.

A room addition can be a great way to add value and space to a home! To get the most bang for the buck, it's great if you have an area that already has a roof, like a porch, that you could close in. It will cost more to start from scratch.

CONSTRUCTION TERMS

Here are a few common construction terms you will want to know if you plan to do an addition to your home.

- **Stud** — Generally used for framing. This is a wooden 2" x 4" (which is actually 1 1/2" x 3 1/2").
- **1x4** — This is a board that is 3/4 inch thick by 3 1/2 inches wide; it is a "nominal" 1 x 4! Usually used for trim work. This is commonly referred to as a "one-by." It could be a 1x2, 1x6, etc.
- **Pressure-Treated Wood** — This is wood that has been soaked in a treatment that makes it hold up better in an exterior environment. It's commonly used for decks or fences. You have to wait for several weeks before staining this, and it will shrink some after it dries.
- **KDAT (Kiln Dried After Treatment)** — This is a pressure-treated board that has been dried in a heated room after it was treated. It can be stained right away and has minimal shrinkage.
- **Particle Board** — Also known as chipboard, this is an engineered wood product made from wood chips and resin. It is inexpensive but does not have much strength and is susceptible to damage when exposed to moisture. Quite a few production cabinets are made with some particle board in them.
- **Gypsum Board** — Also known as drywall or sheetrock, it is a gypsum panel with a paper face on it. This was made to replace lath and plaster that was prevalent in the early 1900s. It comes in different thicknesses although the most common for residential use is 1/2 inch thick. It also comes in a green board, which is moisture-resistant board used for wet areas, like bathrooms. It also comes in a fire-rated board used mostly for commercial jobs.

Robert's Rule #32

Always call before you dig! Call 811 in the US to have utilities located and marked before doing any outdoor digging. This is important because it can save lives, money, and also keep the neighbors from losing their utilities!

FOUNDATIONS

The foundation is a very important element of your project. The type that is chosen depends on what sort of addition or remodel you are planning and the type of foundation you currently have.

Below are explanations of different foundations.

- **Slab** — If your house is on a concrete slab with a level lot, you will probably want to use a slab on grade or monolithic slab. Just as its name suggests, this is a slab of concrete poured over excavated soil and is the least expensive type of foundation to build.
- **Crawl space** — A crawl space is named for the fact that you don't have enough room to stand up in it and sometimes actually have to crawl just to get through it. The existing house and fall of the land will determine how tall the crawl space will need to be. Ideally, you would like three to four feet in height to give you room to work. You want to be sure you get a good French drain put in and make sure it does not become clogged, which can cause flooding in the crawl space.

  It's important to seal the outside of the block to keep water out of the crawl space, and you will also want to put a plastic barrier on the floor of the crawl space.

  If you want to put brick the outside of the crawl space, you will need to pour what's called a brick ledge into the footer.

Basement — A basement addition will be added to an existing basement and will have a framed room above it with a roof above that. Be sure to install a French drain and waterproof the outside really well! In our area of the country, the Southeast, most people use poured concrete for basement walls. You can also use a block wall, but, if you do, it's important to make sure the house is framed and that weight has been put on the wall before backfilling to prevent the wall from pushing over.

Note: A few other things to keep in mind if you do an addition:

- Try to offset the outside walls from the existing wall so the start of the new work isn't obvious. This is especially important if you are trying to match the same brick.
- You might want to use one of the new mini-split HVAC systems to cool the new space instead of trying to extend the ductwork from your existing system.
- Some other obvious things to make sure you consider or identify before doing an addition: property line setbacks, septic tank and lines, utility lines, water flow, entrance into the room from the house, etc.

Sweet Spot — Bedroom Air Conditioner

To keep a master bedroom colder for sleeping, install a small AC unit just for the bedroom. The whole house doesn't have to be cooled, and you will sleep better!

Robert's Replay

We bought a new house in 1988 that had a partial poured concrete wall at the back and down the sides. Shortly after moving in, we had a heavy rain and our downstairs room flooded. The house was still under warranty, so we called the builder and had him come out and take a look at it for us. After doing some digging around, he discovered the ends of the French drain had been covered up by the landscaper and were blocked. Without proper drainage through the pipe, the water ran into the lower part of the house. They uncovered the lines, and we never had a leak after that.

ROOF STYLE

You will want to match the roof of your addition to the existing roof. How that is accomplished depends on how and where the addition meets the existing house. A two-story house with an addition out the back might have enough room for a gable, but many times there is a bedroom window above that would be covered up and won't allow it. The person who does the design of your addition will be able to let you know your options and what their recommendation would be.

> **Capturing more space** — Sometimes a big addition isn't possible for some of the reasons I just mentioned. In these cases, we have to get creative! We start looking for ways to rearrange the layout and maybe capture unused space. Sometimes there is an empty space behind a corner that could be used for additional storage, or a seldom-used adjacent closet that can add just a bit of extra room to your project.

Robert's Replay

I had a client that called me out to remodel four bathrooms in a house that had been built in the late 1970s. There wasn't a lot of room in the master bath. We captured some space from a bedroom closet, but we still needed more room to fit a garden tub. The solution was simple; we extended the bathroom out so that it was even with the roof overhang by extending the floor and adding a header above it. The cost was minimal and the additional 18 inches was just what we needed to make it work.

Robert's Replay

We were installing a master bath vanity, and the homeowner wanted a cabinet that sits on top of the countertop. That part of the bathroom had an angled wall that was about 36 inches wide. I suggested that we might be able to recess it into the wall, so it would not take up as much room on the counter. The area behind the wall turned out to be a dead space, as I suspected, and the recessed cabinet was a great success.

Whenever I am consulting with a client, I first like to listen to what they are thinking. Then, I like to see the available space. We can usually come up with some different ideas for what can be done. The next story is from one of those meetings.

Robert's Replay

I was called out to discuss a major addition for a client. I listened to what his needs were and what he was trying to accomplish. This house had three bedrooms and two baths on the main floor as well as a basement with a bedroom and a bath.

His children were getting to an age where they needed an additional bedroom. I asked about the bedroom in the basement, but he said they have relatives from out of town frequently so that was their guest bedroom. His idea was to add on across the entire back of the house. I looked at this and gave him the projected cost. It was way over his budget. After looking at the house, I asked if he had considered going up into the attic. He had not! After much planning, we added steps to the attic, a large bedroom, a closet, and a window in the gable—all within his budget. Another delighted client!

> *Sweet Spot* — Mudrooms
>
> These can be as big or small as your space allows. You just need a little space for some hooks and a few bins for personal items. Woodwork wall galleries add a cozy feel. Mudroom benches are great to have if you've got the room. A popular piece that we often build is a mudroom bench with a shiplap back, with cubicles under the seat and up above.

Robert's Rule #33

When you need additional space, look for hidden areas that can be claimed as living space—especially attics, porches, under stairways, and dead corners!

Robert's Replay

We have a client we have completed five projects for in a little over a four-year span. The last project was a 600-square-foot addition to the basement, a remodel of the entire first floor, and a completely new kitchen and rear deck.

For one of the earlier projects, they wanted more closet space in the master bedroom. They have a traditional two-story home with the master on the second floor. The garage was on the first floor, and the roof came up beside the master bedroom so there wasn't any room to build out. But, we were able to open a doorway beside the fireplace that came up from the den below. We then added flooring and walls, then insulated, dry-walled, and finished out a nice closet (about 8'x8') within the attic space above the garage. This was about twice the size of their existing closet and was done at a fraction of the cost of an addition!

> *Sweet Spot* — Exposed Beams
>
> Exposed beams continue to be popular and provide a rustic look combined with a traditional feel.
>
> *Sweet Spot* — Tall Bookcases
>
> More people are asking about installing tall bookcases with a rolling ladder, which also adds to the rustic, industrial look.
>
> *Sweet Spot* — Herringbone Patterns
>
> This arrangement of rectangular pieces is used with tile or wood on floors, showers, backsplashes, etc. It is distinguished from the similar chevron pattern by the break in the zigzags.

Sweet Spot — Mixing Colors and Textures

It's becoming common to mix different materials such as natural stones, washed brick, honed granite, natural wood, and beautiful neutral tiles. Colors are often brought in with accent pieces and artwork. The use of shiplap is all the rage now, and wainscoting is still a popular choice with darker ceilings and lighter painted walls.

Jewel tones are also starting to make a comeback, and we're seeing deep navy and burgundy colors as well. You can change your look so easily if you have a natural color background.

Don't be afraid to do something fun! If you change your mind in the years ahead, it's easy to change a paint color to something else.

The Fragment Room

In John, chapter 6, Jesus tells his disciples after feeding 5,000 people to "Gather up the fragments that remain, that nothing be wasted."

This is the foundation of what we call *The Fragment Room*. We have extra cabinet doors. And, after some projects, we have old doors made of good wood that can be re-purposed. We also have a collection of old hardware.

These items are re-purposed into objects and/or works of art by local artists and crafts people. Our proceeds from *The Fragment Room* are designated specifically for charities serving women, children, or families in life-altering and difficult situations.

It's nice to re-purpose something rather than just toss it in the landfill! We also enjoy using reclaimed wood to make islands, vent hoods, countertops, and custom pieces for indoor and porch life. It's awesome to know the wood came from a building that was built over 100 years ago!

Along with The Fragment Room, part of our company's mission is volunteering through community services and events.

CHAPTER 9

LIGHTING AND ELECTRICAL

The lighting you select can make a surprisingly big impact on the look of your new space. There are many choices of lighting and fixtures for different uses. Let's discuss some of the most common ones.

KITCHEN LIGHTING

Under-cabinet lighting is a good choice for task lighting. It illuminates the area where you are working. It also provides effect lighting for times when you are entertaining.

Recessed can lights are very popular in the kitchen. They light up an area of about two to four feet, so you need several of them to light up a room. Most kitchens we see today need at least six to ten of them for adequate lighting. They provide a cleaner look than a big light fixture in the middle of the room.

Many kitchens in new homes are not very well lit. They tend to have dark spots and almost no task lighting! Many of the kitchen remodels we do include under-cabinet lighting and recessed can lights to correct this. I still prefer a small chandelier or decorative light in the middle of the kitchen if there is room. And, we always recommend putting the can lights on a dimmer. The light fixture in the center adds extra light when you need to clean up

Pendant lights give very little light and are mostly for looks. But in the right place, they add a nice design statement to the area. Some say it has the same effect as a woman dressed up with jewelry on. Lighting is like jewelry for your home!

Sweet Spot — Pantry Outlets

Add space and outlets in the pantry for your plug-in appliances, if you have room. Remember to measure length and height to make sure your appliances will fit in the space and allow for easy operation. This is a good option for the microwave if you don't want it mounted in the kitchen. An appliance garage is another popular choice for plug-ins.

Robert's Rule #34

When using recessed can lights in the kitchen, put them on a dimmer switch. This increases their function to allow for full lighting of the area as well as mood lighting when desired.

Special Outlets — There are some instances when you may not want to have an outlet showing on your backsplash. We have some angle bar outlets we can attach to the bottom of a cabinet, just above the tile backsplash and out of sight. They can also include a USB port. These outlet bars can be used under a countertop overhang as well.

BATHROOM LIGHTING

Vanity lighting comes in many varieties. It is commonly installed as a strip light or light bar but can also be a wall-mounted sconce or recessed can lights in the ceiling. The type you choose will depend on the look you are after. But, be careful not to put design over function. Recessed can lights can cast shadows on your face. You might end up looking like you put your makeup on for a theatrical production and not a day at the office!

Showers are usually lighted by a recessed can light with a moisture sealed lens cover. This gives light right where you need it. Some bathrooms have a bullet light which mounts on the wall or ceiling and can be directed toward the area that needs light, such as the tub or shower area.

Overhead lighting adds a nice look and provides good mood lighting. This is usually accomplished with a decorative chandelier or other type of hanging light fixture.

Lora's Replay

Years ago, we had a house where the master bath had two vanities with a knee space connecting them. There were six lights over each vanity and four in the middle. There was also a hanging light in the ceiling. All the lights except the one in the ceiling had been put on the same switch. It was utterly ridiculous! If you needed a light at night, it was so bright you had to close your eyes because it hurt. But if only the ceiling fixture was turned on, it was too dark to see anything.

Robert's Replay

I remember a house I was in one time that had an A-frame ceiling with recessed can lights up on the slopes of the ceiling. The lighting was so poor you needed a lamp on to be able to see. A recessed can light is more of a directional light and only lights up about four feet of floor space. Because of that, it takes more recessed can lights to light up an entire area than it does common ceiling fixtures. So, if you are going to use recessed can lights, make sure you have enough to ensure adequate lighting!

Whenever possible, I try to use LED lights. This technology is very efficient, and the LED bulbs last a long time. They come in different color ranges, so you can choose the one that suits you.

> ### Robert's Rule #35
>
> Try to use LED lights whenever possible. The price of these bulbs has come way down. With the money you will save on electricity and the longevity of these bulbs, it's worth it to invest in changing all the bulbs in your house to LED.

FAMILY/LIVING ROOM LIGHTING

Older homes tended to have switched outlets for lamps and no ceiling lights. That is rare these days. Now, most family room lighting consists of recessed can lights and a ceiling fan, with or without a light kit.

- *Sweet Spot* — Home Comfort Apps

    You can now control your thermostat and lighting through a smart phone app.

- *Sweet Spot* — High, Low, and Hidden Electrical Outlets

    Instead of only installing outlets at the standard 12–18 inches off the floor, put them in baseboards. They blend in and keep the cord at the floor. You can also add them over front doors for wreaths and over the mantle or shelf for the television. Paint them the wall color so they blend in.

BEDROOM LIGHTING

Bedroom lighting can vary quite a bit depending on the size of the room. It's common to have recessed can lights and a ceiling fan with a light kit. If the room has a tray ceiling, it might have trough lighting. It's nice to have lights that shine down onto the bed for reading and can be controlled from each bedside.

Sweet Spot — Docking Drawer

> Add one of these so you have a designated place to charge your phone, iPad, computer, watch, razor, etc. It helps keep cords and power strips neat and out of sight. You may want to also have a USB port mounted in the drawer in addition to the regular outlet.

DINING ROOM LIGHTING

Dining rooms are usually lit by some type of chandelier hanging over the dining table. If the room is large enough, it might also have some recessed can lights, usually on a dimmer. In a long dining room, you might have two large chandeliers over the table!

Lora's Replay

When Robert and I first married, the little house we bought was built in the 1940s and had one electrical socket in the kitchen (maybe not even that, hmm … come to think of it, there may not have been any. I probably had to run an extension cord!). I do know that it was completely insufficient as a working kitchen. Fortunately, there is now a code for placing sockets—they need to be about every three feet at your countertop level. Too many is way better than too few!

Sweet Spot — Picture Lighting

> Highlight your gallery artwork or family portraits with an eyeball or directional light.

Sweet Spot — Desk Printer Drawer

> Add one of these with a plug inside so the printer doesn't sit on top taking up valuable work space.

CHAPTER 10

ROBERT'S REMEDIES

Here are just a few great tips I've picked up along the way:

1. **How to remove stains on ceilings:** This is especially difficult on stippled ceilings or those with sprayed-on acoustical material (popcorn). Take an empty spray bottle and make a 50/50 mix of water and bleach. Make sure to cover flooring, furniture, etc. and anything else that could be damaged by the bleach! Spray the affected area, then take a rag and blot it if it's a bad stain. Otherwise, just soak it really well and let it dry. If it hasn't been painted, the stain will disappear. If it has been painted, you will probably have to paint it again after removing the stain.

2. **Cleaning grout:** A great method for this is to use a mixture of vinegar and baking soda and an old toothbrush. Just apply and use some elbow grease and watch how clean it gets!

3. **Door locks — the key won't go in and out like it is supposed to:** Go to a hardware store and ask for some graphite in a small tube. Stick the tube into the keyhole and spray the graphite into it. Now, insert the key several times. That should distribute the lubricant and allow the lock to function normally again.

4. **Sink faucet has weak pressure:** This can be caused by gunk in the screen filter on the faucet itself. This will usually unscrew (righty-tighty, lefty-loosey), and you can clean it out and re-install it.

5. **Tub drain seems clogged:** This is usually caused by hair getting caught on the drain parts, which then captures soap and more hair until it's eventually clogged. If you have a stopper that turns and closes, you might need to take a screw driver and unscrew the set screw, so you

can remove the stopper. Wear rubber gloves and use a pair of needle nose pliers to start pulling the hair from the drain until you remove it all. After this, you might want to get a drain cover to catch the hair.

6. **Toilet keeps running:** This usually indicates the tank is allowing water to leak out and, as a result, causes the float to go down enough to turn the water on to bring the tank level back up. If the tank has a leak at the base or at the screws, the water will show up on the floor. More common is leaking at the flapper valve, which will show up in the toilet bowl (you can drop dye into the toilet and it will tell you where the leaking is coming from). Unless it's leaking on the floor, the problem can usually be remedied by changing the guts out in the tank.

7. **Kitchen drawer keeps sliding open:** This usually means the rear bracket has come loose, and the tracks are out of level. Remove the drawer, place a level bar on the drawer track to check if it's level. If it's not, loosen the screws on the rear bracket and adjust it up or down until the track is level. This should allow the drawer to stay closed.

8. **Some of your cabinet doors touch each other when you open one of the doors:** How old the doors and hinges on your cabinets are will determine how easy they are to adjust. Essentially you need to adjust the hinges the opposite way, so they don't touch anymore. Newer hinges have a screw you can turn to move the door left and right. Older exposed hinges will be more difficult, but you have to do the same thing. These older doors usually have more room between them, so it would be a rare problem.

9. **The water pressure on the house seems low:** This can be caused by debris clogging the screen on the water pressure valve (where the water enters the house from the street). There is a nut you can loosen, unscrew, and remove, that has a screen filter attached to it. Make sure to turn the water off—either where your water meter is located or where the water comes into the house if you have a shut off there. Take the screen filter and blow out the debris with an air compressor nozzle, then re-install it. If it was clogged up, you will see your water pressure increase dramatically at the faucets throughout the house.

10. **If the electricity goes off:** Save your freezer foods by filling your washing machine with ice. The melting ice just drains out of the machine and keeps your frozen items cold a little longer.
11. **Emergency flood storage:** A dishwasher is great for emergency flood/storm storage of important personal things. It's sturdy because it is located between the cabinets and countertop, and it is waterproof.

THANK YOU

Thank you for taking the time to read this book. Share it with others that you think may benefit from its contents.

Please give us a review and feedback on how this book has helped you.

Robert D. Warren

We can be found at:

    DetailDesign.biz

    DetailCabinetRefacing.com

    YouTube: Detail Design Remodeling

    Facebook: Detail Design and Remodeling

    LinkedIn: Detail Design and Remodeling

    Twitter: @robertremodels

    Instagram: robertremodels

    Kudzu.com: Detail Cabinet Refacing and Remodeling

    Houzz.com: Detail Design and Remodeling

FREE CONSULTATION

Give us a call at

770-379-0446

to schedule a free consultation with our friendly staff for your next project. Customer satisfaction is our #1 priority. Mention this book and receive a free gift.

You may email us at

Admin@DetailDesign.biz.

WE ARE HONORED TO SERVE YOU.

For speaking engagements or coaching, you may contact us through

Robert@RobertDWarren.com

ABOUT THE AUTHOR

Robert was born into a family known for their building expertise. One grandfather had his own sawmill and built homes in ski country. The other grandfather had a custom cabinet shop known for building fine furniture and cabinets for doctors' offices and other establishments. Robert learned from his father and grandfather at an early age and gained the same skills.

Over one thousand homes have been built and remodeled by Robert, and he is sought out for his expertise in the fields of remodeling and cabinet refacing and refinishing. He is a Licensed Residential Contractor for the State of Georgia and a Certified Remodeler (CR) through National Association of the Remodeling Industry (NARI).

Robert is a speaker and coach, and a past host of Kitchen and Bath Radio. He is also a previous Builder Association chapter president and Builder of the Year. His company is the recipient of several awards, including Best of Houzz and Best of Kudzu.

APPENDIX A
HISTORIC NUGGETS FROM THE PAST

OLD KITCHENS

The kitchen started off as a busy hot spot. Since there was no plumbing, water had to be brought in manually. A lot of life revolved around the kitchen since it was a source of heat. The invention of the chimney relieved problems with smoke and soot, and the fireplace chimney became the divider between living rooms and the kitchen. Later, the wood burning stove was developed and became a game-changer!

Robert's Replay

My grandfather had a wood burning stove in the kitchen until the early 1970s. Ranges had been around for many years by that time but, to him, the range couldn't cook cornbread right. So, when they finally did get a range, they moved the wood burning stove to the den so he could continue to cook his cornbread in it. He did this until 103 years old!

The farmhouse sink became popular in the late 19th century and was still the norm in the United States during the 1920s. It was almost always made of cast iron.

The industrial revolution ushered in more efficiency with smaller ovens and tight-fitting appliances that were integrated within cabinetry. It's also around the time that the idea of the golden work triangle was developed. After WWII, with better technology and equipment desired in the kitchen, the more affordable stainless steel sink was devised and became popular.

The 1940s housing boom brought more innovation in the form of things, like ventilation hoods and matching appliances. During the 1960s and 1970s, we saw more interest in cooking and social entertaining. And, by the 1980s, the kitchen had fitted appliances, islands with hanging displays of cookware, and new technologies, like the trash compactor and microwave oven.

This millennium has brought back the popularity of the farmhouse sink. Many people prefer the look along with the ergonomic benefit of not having to reach as far to access the sink. It is also easier to wash larger items like baking sheets and big pots, compared to the standard kitchen sink.

Lora's Replay

My mother was raised in an historic late 1800s home. I have many memories of visiting my grandparents there and can still recall some of the inefficiencies of the home. As was popular in that day, there was the grand hall with a parlor room on each side and a U-shaped staircase at the back. Every room had a huge fireplace in it, but, by the time grandkids came along, none of them were used. Downstairs, gas heaters had been installed in three rooms, but the house had zero insulation. We had to sleep upstairs when we visited, and the temperature was the same as the outside. How miserably cold that was until the invention of the heated blanket! We dressed and undressed under that blanket!

Each room had a single hanging light bulb with exposed wiring running up the wall in the corner of the room. These were turned on by pulling a chain, which made the light sway back and forth.

My grandmother had flowers in troughs that lined the front porch and when my sister and I were grown, each of our 3-year-olds came in with a bouquet of flowers for us—roots and all! That's right, they had pulled up all her flowers!

I motioned to my mom to keep my grandmother diverted while we rushed to re-plant everything like she had it, then I speedily swept up the huge mess! She never said anything, and we certainly never told.

At the end of the porch, a sunroom had been added for storage of fresh vegetables. The front porch had enough rockers for everyone to sit and string green beans. I miss those times, but how thankful I am for heat, electricity, and plumbing! I'm certain some of you have similar memories.

OUTDOOR "PLUMBING"

The outhouse or outdoor bathroom—sometimes referred to as the privy—has been used for years. In the United States, many were still in use in the 1950s. The architectural style varied from a small simple enclosure to fancy brick structures. Most were for single occupancy, but some had three or four "holes."

Privies were typically built away from the house to keep the smell away from the living quarters and also to keep the waste away from the water supply. Before toilet paper was invented, newspapers or magazines were used. When the first patented rolled toilet paper came out in the 1880s, it was usually kept in a covered can to keep mice out. These structures would be moved every year or so, and a new hole dug in the ground.

APPENDIX B

ROBERT'S RULES

Robert's Rule #1

If it's not in writing, it is not clear. Make sure the contract contains everything you discussed. Review the contract before signing. If it's unclear about anything, then have it revised so it covers what you want done, and, only then, should you sign it.

Robert's Rule #2

Never use the contractors' financing [JS1] without first checking on financing from your own bank. Or, pay cash. A twelve-month same as cash deal could cost the contractor hundreds of dollars, and he will charge that into the job and have you think he is doing you a favor.

Robert's Rule #3

Think long and hard before agreeing to a cost-plus contract. It puts the risk of paying too much on the homeowner. It can also give the contractor an incentive to spend more to get a higher percentage. In contrast, a fixed amount contract gives the contractor an incentive not to overspend.

Robert's Rule #4

Never make a decision to use a contractor based on money. Most of the time, you will be wrong. Money is the worst indicator of honesty, integrity, quality of work, a successful project, etc.

Robert's Rule #5

Before signing the deal, ask a contractor the seven most powerful words in the English language—"Is that the best you can do?"

Robert's Rule #6

Negotiate, but be reasonable. Be Nice.

Robert's Rule #7

Talk with your insurance agent before embarking on a new remodeling project. They will make sure you are properly covered.

Robert's Rule #8

Always have your contractor send a copy of insurance coverage directly from the insurance agent. DO NOT accept a photocopy!

Robert's Rule #9

Never start a project on the same day the insurance certificate is issued. The certificate will have the issue date, but it won't go into effect until the next day.

Robert's Rule #10

There is no such thing as a lifetime warranty. (Well, almost never.) If you don't believe me, just read the fine print. Most cabinet lifetime warranties are for seven to ten years.

Ask yourself—if you were selling a product, under what circumstances would you be willing to offer a lifetime warranty? It may only be a sales gimmick.

Robert's Rule #11

Don't use a contractor who doesn't have a good website. It should be more than just a basic website. It should be up to date, mobile optimized, and have enough information about the business to get a feeling about whether you would want to use them. A good website with these items costs money to be maintained and shows commitment to their business.

Robert's Rule #12

It's not how you mess up, but how you recover that counts! Everyone makes mistakes. That's a fact.

When you are doing a multi-faceted project, there is always room for something not to go as planned. A person's character is observed by how they deal with that situation. Don't judge a contractor by a problem that may come up, but by how it gets taken care of. There are many variables, and it may not have been something he did.

Robert's Rule #13

Choose a contractor with experience in the specific type of project that you have. For example, don't choose John's Painting for a kitchen remodel or Joe's Plumbing to complete bathroom renovation. You want every detail done well.

Robert's Rule #14

Never do business with someone you don't like. Even if they have the lowest price—you may live to regret it!

Robert's Rule #15

Do not get too many estimates! It will lead to paralysis of analysis! The estimates are unlikely to include the exact same products or solutions, and too many can get overwhelming.

Robert's Rule #16

A true professional will spend time listening to what you have to say.

Robert's Rule #17

When setting up the first meeting for a sales consultation, note how this initial part of the process goes. First impressions can be very telling. It might help you decide whether or not to use them later on.

Robert's Rule #18

Be courteous! If you need to reschedule an appointment, call the salesperson. If you cannot reach them, call the company directly. Do for them what you would want them to do for you!

Robert's Rule #19

If you are creatively challenged, then make sure you hire the services of someone who can help you with ideas and viable options. Someone who can help you with aesthetic and color options. I have worked with many decorators and designers who turn out great work and are usually reasonably priced.

Robert's Rule #20

At the end of each visit, always set up the next appointment day and time and agree about the purpose of the next meeting and its anticipated outcome.

Robert's Rule #21

Caution: Don't give a subcontractor money upfront. Only pay in full when a project is completed.

A general contractor is licensed and insured and is usually well established. For general contractors, it is standard to get an upfront deposit and additional payments throughout the project.

Robert's Rule #22

Zig Ziglar used to say, "You can't make a good deal with a bad guy." Character matters!

Robert's Rule #23

Make sure the refrigerator has a countertop within reach, on the side of the door opening. A double door refrigerator is good on either side. The best scenario is having an island in front of it also.

Robert's Rule #24

Before choosing soft-close drawer glides, consider who will be using them. If an elderly person or someone with arthritis will be using them, you may want to reconsider. Since the mechanism works by "cocking a trigger" when the drawer is first opened, it may be difficult for some because it requires extra resistance.

Robert's Rule #25

When choosing hardware, try to avoid a knob that is square or straight lined. They will constantly be turning out of level or plumb and will bother you every time you see them.

Robert's Rule #26

When selecting drawer pulls, beware of pulls that stick out on each side. They can catch clothing and stretch or tear it!

Robert's Rule #27

If the house is old and you have a bathroom that is original, your best option may be to restore it back to its original glory instead of tearing it out and doing a complete update.

Robert's Rule #28

Always use a cement backer board under your tile when setting on a wood floor system. This will help provide a stronger tile floor and will help prevent cracks and loose tiles due to poor adhesion.

Robert's Rule #29

When installing a mud-set pan over vinyl liner in a tile shower floor, be sure your installer knows how to install a pre-bed under the vinyl liner.

Robert's Rule #30

When installing an exhaust fan in a bathroom, it's usually a good idea to wire it so it turns on with the bathroom light or, in a larger bathroom, have it come on with the shower light.

Robert's Rule #31

Always keep your pets secured and out of the way during construction—for their safety and the workers'. Bonus: It keeps pet hair from getting stuck in fresh paint!

Robert's Rule #32

Always call before you dig! Call 811 in the US to have utilities located and marked before doing any outdoor digging. This is important because it can save lives, money, and also keep the neighbors from losing their utilities!

Robert's Rule #33

When you need additional space, look for hidden areas that can be claimed as living space—especially attics, porches, under stairways, and dead corners!

Robert's Rule #34

When using recessed can lights in the kitchen, put them on a dimmer switch. This increases their function to allow for full lighting of the area as well as mood lighting when desired.

Robert's Rule #35

Try to use LED lights whenever possible. The price of these bulbs has come way down. With the money you will save on electricity and the longevity of these bulbs, it's worth it to invest in changing all the bulbs in your house to LED.